All About You
In the Creative Circle
by
Ardys U. Reverman, Ph.D.

No. 1

In the Creative Circle of Learning

"To understand our lives as lifelong opportunities of learning is to claim the spiritual road into wholeness." **The Right Reverend Rustin Kimsey, The Episcopal Bishop of Eastern Oregon**

"This work makes it easy and natural for child and adult to get back into the communication and understanding mode so that everyone in the family can be comfortable and accepted."
Lendon H. Smith, M.D. ,author *The Children's Doctor.*

"I am pleased to be able to add my support to the work you are doing in the latest brain research that offers a new and exciting body of knowledge to the field of education."**Anthony R. Palermini,Ph.D. Superintendent, David Douglas School District, Oregon.**

"Diversity means families in *everyday* relationships. For real success learn to understand differences where everybody counts."
Nickyanne Laman, Founding Sales Director, Discovery Toys.

"To appreciate each others talents on the whole team leads to championships, skillfully playing our own part well with others."
Bobby Harris, Athletics Coach, Jefferson High School, Oregon.

"Understanding how people process information from different perceptual positions, aids us with important skills we use all our lives." **Susan Hammer, Attorney,Stoel, Rives, Boley, Jones &Grey.**

"Each of us is becoming more conscious of our own creative purpose. This will enhance the greater collective creativity."
John Nance, author of *The Gentle Tasaday.*

"Conscious choices and unconscious forces bring an idea whose marketing time has come; You Knowing You, a niche to be met."
Lynda Falkenstein, Ph.D., author of *Nichecraft.*

"When I meet a skilled person in any field, I know they are using their whole brain creatively, productively with a sense of humor."
Ben Rushford, D.D.S., Reconstruction Dentistry, O. H. S. Center.

"If we see intelligence as our only edge, we must learn to change, using it better."**Carol Qutub, teacher and Doctoral Candidate.**

"A sense of humor and laughter keeps your head listening to your heart fulfilling your sense of paradox, health and balance in life."
Diane (Dicey)Delbrueck Brinck, 1992 Chrmn, Amer.HrtAsso.Ball.

"Natural talent is learning to control and continue to develop your own essentials of high self-esteem and peak productivity."
Chris Cusick, President, Cusick's Talent Agency.

"The cornerstone of effective management and the number one edge over competition is that people must like you and trust you. In a competitive world the edges are extremely important."
Bill Reilly, President, William Reilly Engineering.

"The inner game of business is personal creativity. A valuable tool to help us to develop successful marketing skills."
Helen M. Rockey, General Manager, Nike, Inc.

"Help young people to discover within the strength, enthusiasm and wisdom of their own motivations as the best natural high."
Janet Corson, PastPres, American Medical Association Wives.

"Creativity empowers great art when our hearts and minds are touched by the human soul." **Charlotte Lewis, Artist**

"The best fitness value for families and businesses is the ability to be a flexible communicator. By recognizing and working with differences we create healthy futures for all." **Douglas Houser, Attorney, Bullivant, Houser, Bailey, Pendergrass & Hoffman.**

Listening to your customer-centered needs ensures a Win/Win investment benefit for all." **Wm. Barendrick Jr.,Past.Pres.O.A.R.**

"To avoid loss of potential natural ability it is so simple, yet powerful to uncover, encourage and develop talents at an early age ." **Susan Murche,Educators for Social Responsibility**

"Craft is that part of the art that can be predicted, taught, and repeated. This is because story structure is dictated by human nature." **Gary Provost, Award Winning Author Childrens Books**

"Masculinity is doing, femininity is thinking and feeling the natural whole body system." **Lupe Rushford, Jen-Shin Practitioner**

"This is an ultimate leading edge insight into customer service that makes all other previous information obsolete." **Lloyd Warren, Vice President, In-Flight Services, Northwest Airlines.**

"Parents and professionals are most effective by supporting and valuing teamwork. We shine at feeling really good about what we like to do that works. This makes a parents vital role credible." **Carlita and Ron Evezich, Evezich Enterprises.**

"When pulling a garment together we start the creative process with color, followed by silhouette; engineering of technique and measurement completes the style. This is a whole brain process." **John H. Herman, President, Duffel Sportswear.**

" Rethinking competition gives us "no-cost/low-cost" fixes that will make a difference and can be implemented immediately." **Mike Falkenstein, Juvenile Court Referee.**

"Analyzing scripts, changing directors' minds to improve production, uses the brain in a way so that every part counts." **Gordon Kee, Production Manager, Orion Pictures.**

"We must increase input to the brain by taking on new tasks, in order to increase the neural structure and keep our brains healthy." **Cameron Truesdell, President, LTCInc., Long Term Health Care**

"Every one I work with feels empowered by having this snapshot of their natural motivations. Understand how you and your child think." **Paul Lyons, CEO, Centerplace Publishing Company.**

"I am proud to recommend Ardys Reverman to you for a spot on the National Convention Program. I have received glowing reports from realtors who have attended her NLP seminars around the country. Get her book." **Vicki Kilgore, Ed. Dir., M A R**

"Thinking is the ultimate human resource; we continue to re-discover brilliant new methods to tackle any problem." **Phil Underwood, Engineer.**

"Flexibility is priority in the process of gathering information creating mutually satisfying benefits for all parties." **Jack Reverman, President, Reverman Associates**

All About You
In the Creative Circle
by
Ardys U. Reverman, Ph.D.

Illustrated by
Charlotte Lewis

No. 1

TAPROOTS PRESS
3503 SW Gale Avenue
Portland, Oregon 97201

Copyright © 1993 by Ardys U. Reverman

All rights reserved. No part of this book may be reproduced or distributed in any form or by any means without the prior written permission of the publisher.

Printed in the United States of America
First edition February 1993

Library of Congress Cataloging in Publication Data
Reverman, Ardys U.
All About You/In the Creative Circle
Summary: An adult/child interactive book to help children develop understanding, self-respect and control of their creative temperament style in their own way.
p. 223 cm.
1. Self-respect —Juvenile literature. 2. Self-perception — Juvenile literature. 3. Success—Psychological aspects. 4. Child development. 5. Temperament. 6. Parental acceptance. 7. Cognition I Title.

BF697.5.S54.R   1993
158.1   20   92—90748
                     CIP
ISBN 0-9625385-3-1

Trademark information: Think-about Owl™, Look-about Lion™, Talk-about Chimp™, Feel-about Koala™, Synergy Pals™, Friendly Universe Series™ and Taproots Productions™ are registered trademarks of Ardys U. Reverman and may not be reproduced in whole or in part in any form. Copyright © 1987. All rights reserved.

VI

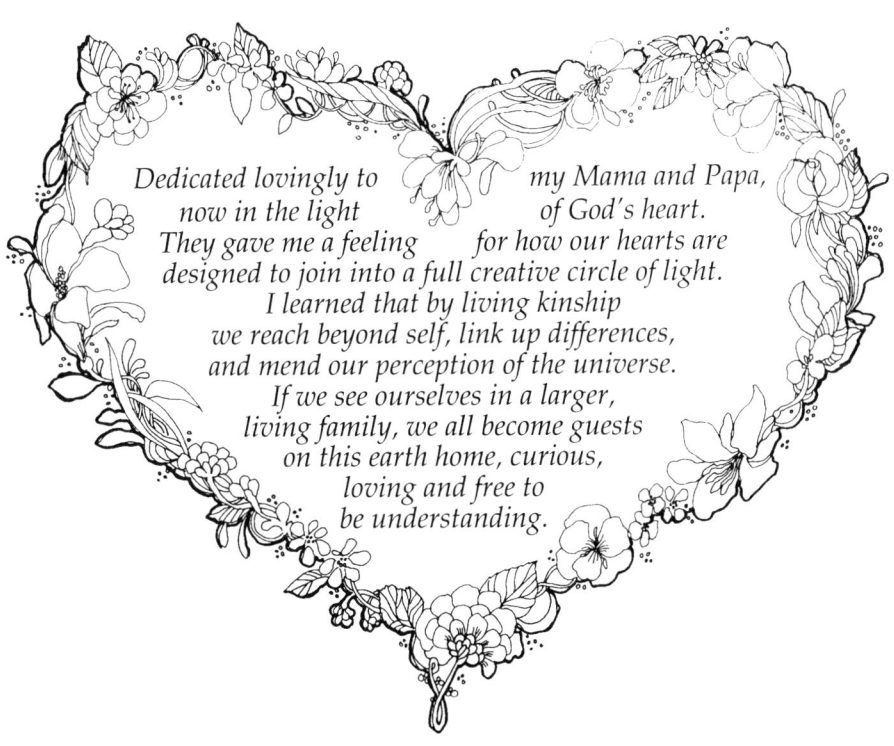

*Dedicated lovingly to my Mama and Papa,
now in the light of God's heart.
They gave me a feeling for how our hearts are
designed to join into a full creative circle of light.
I learned that by living kinship
we reach beyond self, link up differences,
and mend our perception of the universe.
If we see ourselves in a larger,
living family, we all become guests
on this earth home, curious,
loving and free to
be understanding.*

Agreement of Collaboration

TAPROOTS PRESS has designed this material to provide information in regard to the subject matter covered. It is sold with the understanding that the publishers and authors are not liable for the misconception or misuse of information provided. Every effort has been made to make this information as complete and as accurate as possible. The purpose of this information is to educate. The author and TAPROOTS PRESS shall have neither liability nor responsibility to any person or entity with respect to any loss, damage, or injury caused or alleged to be caused directly or indirectly by the information contained herein. They shall also not be liable for the completeness or accuracy of the contents of the books and products in this friendly universe series.

Acknowledgments
My Own Family Tree

Every tree needs a good soil in which to grow deep taproots and gather nourishment for supple strength to bend and bow. The soil from which this book grew is deep and rich, the insights of many who have studied the human mind, and the unconscious mind that was always there. It has been the work of the brave side of the brain, by those curious and courageous in every culture. Their mysteries began in ancient times with the search for the god within, and continue with the work of scientists and natural philosophers. Each discovery suggests another possibility, and new discoveries are made.

Today this is carried forward through synergy. We are the first generation to be aware of itself as a whole, a new form of joining what we do best. We will create much more together than anything we could do alone. This shift is away from a judgmental or mechanistic view towards a discernment of a living system. Like the growth of a tree, the rings compress towards the core as each ring of life is added. The past is not lost, just rooted in an emotional creative core of planetary interdependence. We realize now that evolution is not synonymous with material progress and that we continually create our world in a personal way, based on creativity, not domination. We are looking within ourselves for deeper levels of awareness defined by creativity, not gender. This gives us an understanding to honor the fit of the natural attraction we have for each other. The means, as well as ends, goals are insights of larger lessons in our cognitive awareness. A "flat world" may be a social belief and seem real. What happens when that belief becomes dysfunctional in the light of fact? When we see only a small piece of the earth at one time it looks flat because it is big and we are small. Our mind either locks us into a limited "flat world view" or jumps beyond the fear of the unknown, stretching beyond our own world view to include new possibilities and paradoxes when we pay attention to how other people learn, in a collective core.

As Alfred Korzybski reminds us, "The map (our experience) is not the territory (the world)." Each of us perceives a different and equally real reality. A life that is truly lived is filled with interactions that help the individual know who he or she is — to explore their reality, to question it, stretch its boundaries and move around the whole circle of learning. Einstein's theory of relativity has helped us discover the benefits of a totally connected universe. To relate better, we need to have a mental framework to link with people and have direct access to their talents — the law of synergy. Conscious choices are being formed by unconscious forces, just as we notice time/space changes things and people change right along with them.

My roots, and the roots of this book, come from a mixture of frustration, patience and curiosity. A baby has a brain but little knowledge. When we begin our life, we understand almost nothing about our world and its values. As old beliefs collapse and new ones take their place, we move our boundaries towards new worlds of interdependence. My belief that all problems have solutions comes from my first role models. My mother, Ella Hellmann Urbigkeit, with her immigrant's mind full of hope and determination, fulfilled her character, against cultural gender type, by becoming a builder. My father, Edward Charles Urbigkeit, expressed his sweet character in music and a capacity for empathy. Their root values resulted in different ways of approaching the wonder of life, working and belonging together. Unable to voice this or negotiate values that were deeply connected to their motivations made understanding each other difficult.

They had no information about temperament types or emotional needs. The society they lived in was more rigid about gender expectations. Wisdom is the best leader, not gender, culture, race or age. They longed to love one another and found a way to work together intuitively, a struggle that was not easy for them or their children. I had no doubt about their love and respect for one another. The childhood support of my brothers, Eldon, Oliver and Stanley, are memories from the long past. I feel their warm support in a timeless way and continue to learn from them.

The roots of my life and work grew into a strong trunk of emotional support from longtime friends and colleagues who, in living, have provided the material which became this book. Heartfelt thanks to Emelia Rathbun, who defined the wise concept of right relationship (living your own life on purpose), and to Eva Vasiljevic, my spiritual mother, who has always given me her unconditional love. "Love survives when wisdom has an effective voice."

As this book grew, so the trunk of nourishment and support branched into new and diverse relationships. I am especially grateful to illustrator Charlotte Lewis, who made my dream pictures become real in a different language of the brain. Seoni Baird lent a mindful heart to shape and organize a vast body of raw and rich information into a coherent whole. Karen Lewis contributed some of the wonderful poems. Bill Johnson helped me to initially organize and structure the content. Andrea Nichols, Sharon Lowrie and Carlene Lynch tied up a lot of loose ends. Carol Qutub provided a room with an ocean view where I could work. Sarah Parker and Patti Ford helped with teacher strategies. Larry Fry, Sally Cumming, David Wagner, Chris Nielsen, Todd Schomer and Ryan Manwiller helped along the way. Milla Walker, Beth Klug, Lorraine Stratton and Duane Ransom with Arbor Graphics fine-tuned the end product.

I have drawn special nourishment from the work of those who are constantly alert for new brain/mind information. Many people gave me the gift of their time, willing to talk and contribute their insight to enrich this work: Ed and Sharon Beall, Carman and Tom Beatty, Elmira and Cloudy Beyer, Judy Binder, Margot Brown, Dee Madden Campbell, Pat Chandler, John and Janet Corson, Wes Cropper, Robert Dilts, Marilyn Easley, Susan Hammer, Dean Jacobs, Kris Kelly, Vicki Kilgore, Mary and Daryll Klein, Nicky Laman, Trish Laufenberg, Eric Lepire, Hal Leskinen, Cheryl Livneh, Linnel Littke, Helen and Paul Lyons, Heather Masaitis, Susan and Don Murche, John Nance, Tony Palermini, Leonora and Bob Perron, Gail Pollock, Helen Rockey, Rosemary Squires, Linda and Michelle Steen, Karen Swallow, Katja and Julia Ubbelohde, Laura Weaver, and the Vasiljevic family. My colleagues and students at Portland State University continually remind me that feelings of self-respect and mutual-respect are really necessary for everyone's creative temperament to expand the service's they offer in this network. My personal growing edge, always stretching towards new experience, is my family — my wholehearted children, Peter, Alex and Liza and my husband, Jack, who opened me to the unfolding mystery of human creativity, all of us growing, in endless curiosity, toward this book. They helped me grasp the significance of shared experience, the deeply-rooted connections necessary for a family to love and learn from each other. And now my daughter-in-law, Kristin, is showing me the mystery of kinship anew. The basic attraction of love brings particles of life together to form bodies of ever greater complexity. Our expected grandchild reminds me of the miracle that we start our lives inside another human and how truly we are made to interact with each other.

Like the miracle of life, love renews itself over and over again. To my family, I express love and appreciation. Family reveals the secrets of personality, laughing and crying together through shared mistakes and successes. Every crisis presents the paradox of choice: the defense of safety or the opportunity to change and grow. It is an adventure in forgiveness for ourselves and others as we learn and understand how to call each other "beloved." I draw from these soils of inspiration and these springs of love as they continue to bring me into being. An ecology of souls reflects the ecology of nature; nature needs everyone's genius to improve this planet a little more for our grandchildren, the

timeless faces yet to be conceived.

This is how the book grew; this is how I grow, finding the courage to stretch my own growing edge, again and again.

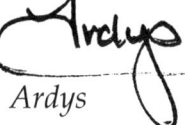
Ardys

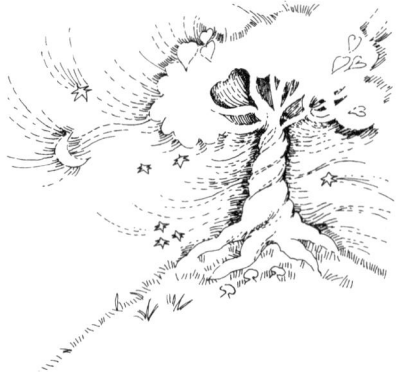

Foreword

It is very difficult to put emotions and feelings into words, not just for children, but for us mature, wise adults. There is no doubt that we could learn better skills to communicate with our children and each other. While animals smell each other, humans guess another's emotions by what is shown on the face: Anger, love, boredom, anxiety, fear, pain, etc. We can do the Haim Ginott strategy of "I see you are angry. Can you tell me about it?" But who remembers what to ask when one is tired or distracted?

We also know that people are different; some are hyper, some are calm and collected, some learn by doing, some learn by hearing or feeling or reading. We are all different. Dr. Reverman has captured those differences in this work and made it easy and natural for child and adult to get back into the communication and understanding mode so that everyone in the family can be comfortable and accepted. Once that has happened, parents can give their children a good self-image, which is the chief job of childhood: Acquire a positive self-concept, so that when that child matures, he/she will be a contributing, worthwhile adult.

Lendon H. Smith, M.D.

Think-about Owl knows your need for order and doing things the right and safe way.

Look-about Lion knows your need for freedom and doing things your own way.

Feel-about Koala knows your need for harmony and doing things easily together.

Talk-about Chimp knows your need for understanding and doing things in a new and fun way.

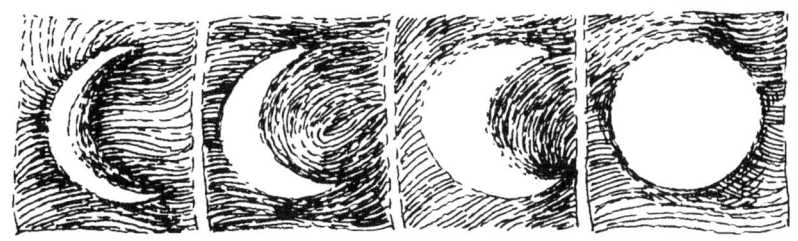

Preface
An Important Message To Parents and Other Adventurers

If you are reading this, you probably have some concerns about the future of our children. Perhaps you are fearful about the impact of our changing society and how to prepare children for the future. Perhaps your concern is for a specific child and individual problems you foresee. Whether your concerns are global or specific you already have an emotional commitment to creating a better future for the children of today.

As a parent, teacher and learner for thirty years, I have been fascinated by some basic questions: How do we learn? How do we know things intuitively? How do we think creatively?

Our children will inherit a new world of connections. This brave new world will operate through our understanding of how natural dynamic processes work. New belief systems are constantly created, evolving into a new understanding of the nature of things. In this new world of quantum physics where a beam of light can be seen as either a particle or wave, we realize the idea of living with paradox. Our children must learn to be curious and comfortable about things that change swiftly and things that remain unknown and unanswerable. They must discover for themselves the true meaning behind appearances. Everything in this universe is alive, unique and interrelated and we learn through direct, original participation with it. Meaning is virtually synonymous with context. It is in relation to other things and, especially, other people that we "know" anything. Each of us is unique and offers someone else a new and different perspective on life. One mode of "knowing" need not conflict with another; rather, they truly complement one another. In our children's future, we may realize that we are one world, one living society, particles of a single system, a dynamic interaction of multiple parts. When we realize that this diversity is an intelligent system with all the involvement and information self-correcting, we can embrace the diversity instead of repressing it.

We have been taught so many things that "just aren't so" but we must determine what works for ourselves. We can do this with a little help from brain/mind research. Learning occurs throughout the entire brain when we are alert, relaxed and feel safe; we learn more and retain it. When changes are approached naturally and pleasurably, we have much better results for both the intrapersonal intelligence (knowing who we are) and the interpersonal intelligence (helping each other). In addition, an intelligent approach to ourselves and the world is more important to our health, and that of the world, than all the fitness programs and reforms we might undertake. Think about your own youth. Consider the suffering of being ignored, misunderstood or falsely accused. Consider the effect of wearing a mask, trying to be someone we are not, trying to please while losing hope of expressing what feels most natural to give. The language of the heart is the body's response to free dialogue with the world; your head listens to your heart. This happens by integrating all the capable logical, feeling, expressive and organizational parts within. On the other hand, if we become too polarized in our personal temperament and expression, we lose choice and can spend a lifetime seeking for and conflicting with our polar opposite. Consider how people are so often attracted to their opposite temperament type — the orderly with the spontaneous, the agreeable with the controlling, the reflective with the expressive, the exacting with the generalizing. By understanding temperament we can develop sensitivity and tolerance both inside and outside. We acquire a great deal of practical, physical knowledge about our world, and yet the healthy changes will come from knowing our emotional "triggers" — being able to speak a language of the heart. For example, our weaknesses are strengths exaggerated — too much spontaneity may neglect the order we need in our lives.

Our children have more information available than any previous generation. Often, they see the present and the future more clearly than we do. Learning techniques are inadequate when they do not reinforce what our children want and need to know from their natural way of being, for their emotional core of interests. This is what the study of temperament types is all about. We understand now that a tense child who does not learn well in a compartmented, fact-based format may actually lose potential by not using his or her natural intelligence effectively. By uncovering talents at an early age and encouraging development of these natural gifts this can be avoided.

If you are a parent, you are your child's most important teacher. One fact of being a parent is inescapable: Our children, on a conscious or subconscious level, are constantly observing and measuring our responses to life. Genes are for keeps, but our brains mimic to learn. The brain is designed to interact with support and assistance. We need a safe emotional environment in order to bond in communication with others; through that interaction of the heart we have purpose and from that we can bring together all the parts within, a unity which is genius in a very real sense. Parents who recognize that their potentially capable child is not thinking or acting "smart" cannot help but feel sad, frustrated, stressed and even resentful. For both parents and concerned educators, watching a child waste precious potential and make flawed decisions is a heart-wrenching ordeal.

Our natural inclination is to help our children. Unfortunately, this desire to intervene is frequently misunderstood and ends in arguments, withdrawal and alienation. We may speak the same language, but understanding how to satisfy the needs of the heart comes from learning to speak each other's *emotional* language. This language of our brain determines how we think about and interpret the world of relationship around us. The more we understand just how we think and learn, about temperament type, the more we can contribute to the intellectual and emotional development of our children and to healthy, joyful relationships with them. Our thoughts generate wants, motives and values; these are expressed as feeling needs which lead to patterns of action. When temperament type remains unknown or unacknowledged and feeling needs cease to be met, the individual is an enigma inside and outside, constantly flip-flopping between miserable isolation and clinging overcompensation, locked into a lifetime of inappropriate behavior patterns. Though a temperament type may be masked for years, ultimately and unconsciously the true temperament will manifest itself. Often, this occurs with disastrous results — like uncorking a genie from a bottle. By knowing a child's temperament type we can understand the causes of a child's actions most of the time. When we know this we can help the child to understand his or her temperament type and to associate values and feeling needs with action. Though an adult and child may be of different temperament types, it is the fit, not the type, that determines the course of the child's development. The need we all have is to learn what we are good at and where we fit in. We are happiest when we recognize what we were born to do best and develop these gifts for success and self-fulfillment.

All About You is an interactive "journey of self-discovery." Intended, primarily, for sharing between parent and child, it can also be used by grandparents or other family members, educators, or any caring adult. Sharing this journey of self-discovery in a mindful and heartfelt way can create a special communication and life-enhancing bond. To derive full benefit from *All About You: In the Creative Circle,* you must be willing to work together on the profile and activities. Encourage your child to color their book. This will make it personal for them as a thought-provoking, fun and shared exploration of the self and each other. This book is a message that we are designed to work and play in partnership.

The four animal characters of *All About You: In the Creative Circle* represent learning styles, living styles and emotional styles, and help us pull some abstract ideas into a knowable form. The book is designed around the four animals' traits: To draw the step-by-step thinking process of the Owl, the hands-on practice of the Koala, the talking-together-about-it of the Chimp and the listening-to-meaning-behind-the-words synthesis of the Lion. The sharing and examination of thoughts and feelings forms a model for the larger synergy of all our interrelationships.

Knowing that our words and deeds influence the attitudes, thoughts, skills and values of our children puts us in a position of monumental responsibility. This is a message for their future. The ecological crisis and the cultural transformation we are now experiencing are spiritual turning points for all people. To understand our place in creation is to honor diversity in all living things.

Love and Laughter,
Ardys

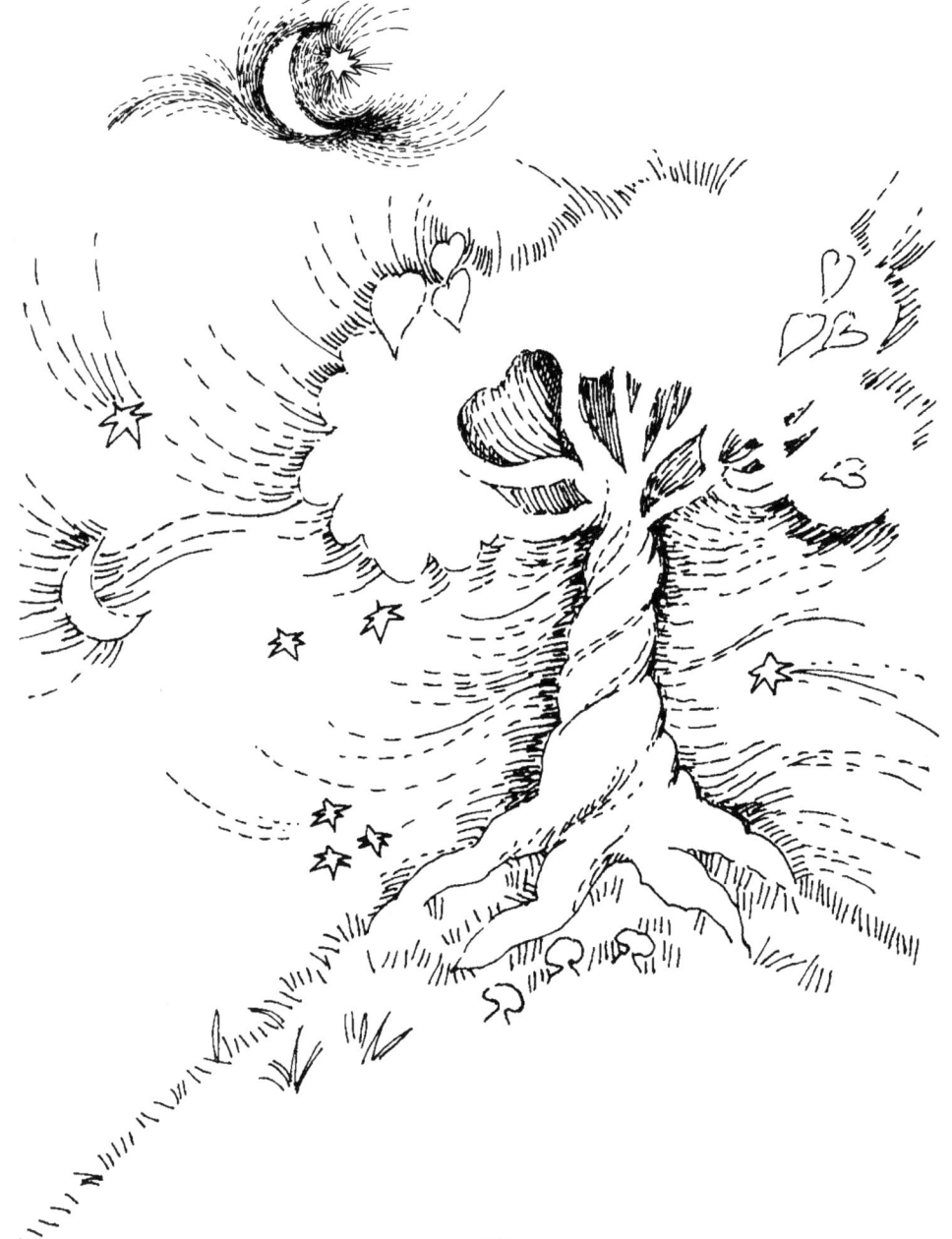

XX

"*A poem in a child there always is to be. A poem in a child is always to go free.*"

Liza Reverman
Age 8

"Words heal the feelings of memories in the heart."

A Child

Table Of Contents

In the Creative Circle of Learning II
Dedication VII
Acknowledgment IX
Foreword XIII
Preface XV
The Inside Story 1
The Four Kinds of You Inside 5
Discover Your Natural Talents 11
Your Heart-Wood Center 20
Just Like a Tree 29
The Think-about Owl 43
The Look-about Lion 53
The Talk-about Chimp 63
The Feel-about Koala 73
Discover Your Deeply-Rooted Values 83
Working Together as Synergy Pals 87
How Each is a Part of the Whole 103
The Seven Stretches 105
Stretching Your Growing Edge 123
Important Words for Adults 130
Recommended Reading for Adults 132

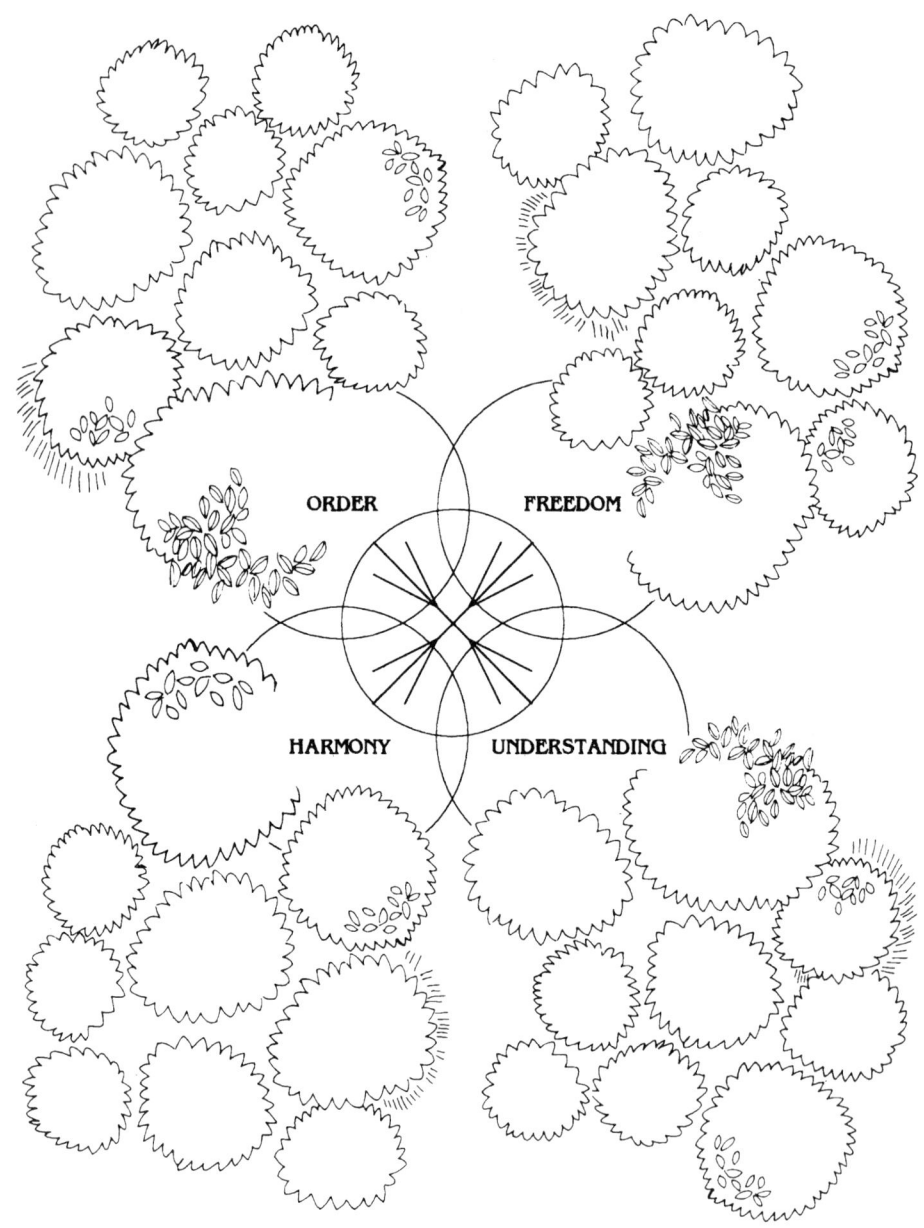

"*We dance 'round the ring and suppose, but the secret sits in the middle and knows.*"

Robert Frost

this book belongs to

_____

As part of the new teamwork mind

*"They each give their best
to all of the rest with
each as part of the whole."*

Color this book in your own natural way

The Inside Story

Who are YOU in your heart?

If you could look inside yourself
through a magic window
what do you suppose you'd see?

You'd see
the different parts
of your personality
that make you a whole person
with a mind of your own.

The magic window is like a prism
that shows the colors of the lights Inside.

When you look through the magic window,
you'll see the colors:
green, blue, yellow, and red
have become four friendly animals.

These animals are the
colors, seasons and moods.
They're different ways of looking at the world.
Your thoughts color your
own inner map and your point of view.

They're just another way
of looking at the different parts
inside of **YOU**.

You'll see a little bit of yourself
in each one of the
four animals.

As you learn more about them,
your heart may tell you
that one of the four
is more like **YOU**
than the others
and more special to you.

Which one is most like **YOU**?
Ask your heart and then imagine . . .
What were you born to do best?

The Magic Window to the Inside of you

The Four Kinds of You Inside

Which part is most like **You?**

When you imagine yourself as a . . .

Think-about Owl,

Look-about Lion,

Talk-about Chimp,

Feel-about Koala

Which one is most like **YOU?**
At different times, you'll see a part of each in you.
Now you can stretch to the part least like you
to see yourself with new eyes, taking
responsibliity within yourself to
develop more usefulness.

Am I someone who likes to sit in my room where I feel safe as I quietly think and work by myself? Do I like to carefully figure things out and put everything in order?

Through my Think-about window, I know how to gather details and plans and to keep order and safety.

Am I a Think-about Owl, who likes to be safe at home, and have things in order and time to think?

Am I someone who likes to have
choices and make quick decisions?
Am I able to work out a plan in my
mind and get results in any project
that I choose?

Through my Look-about window,
I see a world to explore and the result
of having the freedom to take charge.

Am I a Look-about Lion who likes to get
results, have a zillion choices and be a
free spirit?

Am I someone who likes to share
ideas, listen and talk, have hunches
in bunches and be the one who loves
to have fun?

Through my Talk-about window,
I share inspired ideas and dreams.
I know how to understand others
and be understood.

Am I a Talk-about Chimp who likes to
listen and talk about ideas and have
understanding?

Am I someone who loves to make
and touch things? And when I know
everyone around me is friendly, do I
like to share my feelings and talk?

Through my Feel-about window,
I feel how to create harmony; especially
how to help friends get along with me.

Am I a Feel-about Koala who likes to
touch things, feel in harmony and be
with my friends?

Most people consider themselves to be a
Think-about, Look-about, Talk-about, or Feel-about
kind of person most of the time.

Each part has its own natural talents
and a certain way of being in the world.

We are really at our best
when we bring all the parts together,
Outside and Inside ourselves.

Understanding Your Natural Talents
and
What You're Willing to Do That's Important to YOU

And now for a little quiz:
it's not a ~~test~~, though.
The only thing you have to know
is something about yourself.
It will help you discover
the way you like most to be,
the urges and actions
you like to take in the world,
understanding more
about your own natural talents.

There's an overall pattern
in the center core of your own well-being
that tells you what you're willing to do, and
how to make sense
of each other's behavior,
because each fills a part of the whole.

*"Order, Freedom, Understanding and Harmony
turn the creative circle of values connecting us all
in the Friendly Universe,
and it continues on and on."*

Take some time to think about
and answer the following questions.
They'll tell you what you want to know.

Answer the questions
according to the very strongest feelings you have
about each one.

This is the easiest and most natural way
for you to understand the creative circle
of your own deeply-rooted values —
(Order, Freedom, Understanding, Harmony)
— how you like to feel and act
and how you think, see, hear and feel.

Because we usually choose
what is most true for us,
our quiz answers are always correct.

Because other people have different talents
and think, see, hear and feel things differently,
they will answer the questions differently.

After you have finished the quiz,
you may find it interesting and fun
to talk about your different answers
with your friends.

For each question, consider how you really, honestly feel about each of the 4 answers.

Give a four (4) to the answer most like you.
Give a three (3) to the answer next most like you.
Give a two (2) to the answer next to least like you.
Give a one (1) to the answer least like you.

Here's an example of how to answer the questions:

I like . . .

* to have my things in **order** the right way.	2	The answer next to least like me.
* the **freedom** to do things my own way.	1	The answer least like me.
* the **harmony** of belonging with my friends the happy way.	4	The answer the most like me.
* **understanding** my ideas and dreams a new way.	3	The answer next most like me.

1. I feel happy with myself when I am . . .

a. helping my friends get along together
and being thanked for my help ....

b. putting my belongings in order
so I can find things when I need them ....

c. sharing my new ideas which excite
others into seeking solutions ....

d. picturing a plan and explaining
how to get it done quickly and correctly ...

2. I work best when I can . . .

a. work with others and be shown how
to do things by someone who knows how ...

b. think and work quietly on my own,
following directions step-by-step ....

c. watch what someone does well, plan
how I will do it, and get it done ....

d. tell others my new ideas, inspiring them
to risk doing things in a new way ....

Add up the numbers going down in each column of boxes. Put the total in the matching box at the bottom of the page.

14

3. When I'm with others talking and listening, I ...

a. first watch and listen, then feel free to explain the plan I see and what to do ....

b. first enthusiastically tell my new ideas, then I want to hear if they understood me ....

c. warmly ask about their feelings and share my feelings in a friendly, helpful way ....

d. just politely listen until I'm asked what I think, then I quietly answer ....

4. I like stories ...

a. about real-life problems with feelings that go a little deeper and end happily (*Shiloh / Sarah, Plain and Tall*) ....

b. about true adventure, useful clues, facts, and skilled, tried & true hero/ines (*The Other Side of the Mountain / Sadako*) ....

c. about great brains from history that look a little further into tomorrow (*Helen Keller / Star Wars*) ....

d. that discover magical things, faraway places, and people with different beliefs (*A Wrinkle in Time / Wizard of Oz*) ....

Add up the numbers going down in each column of boxes. Put the total in the matching box at the bottom of the page.

15

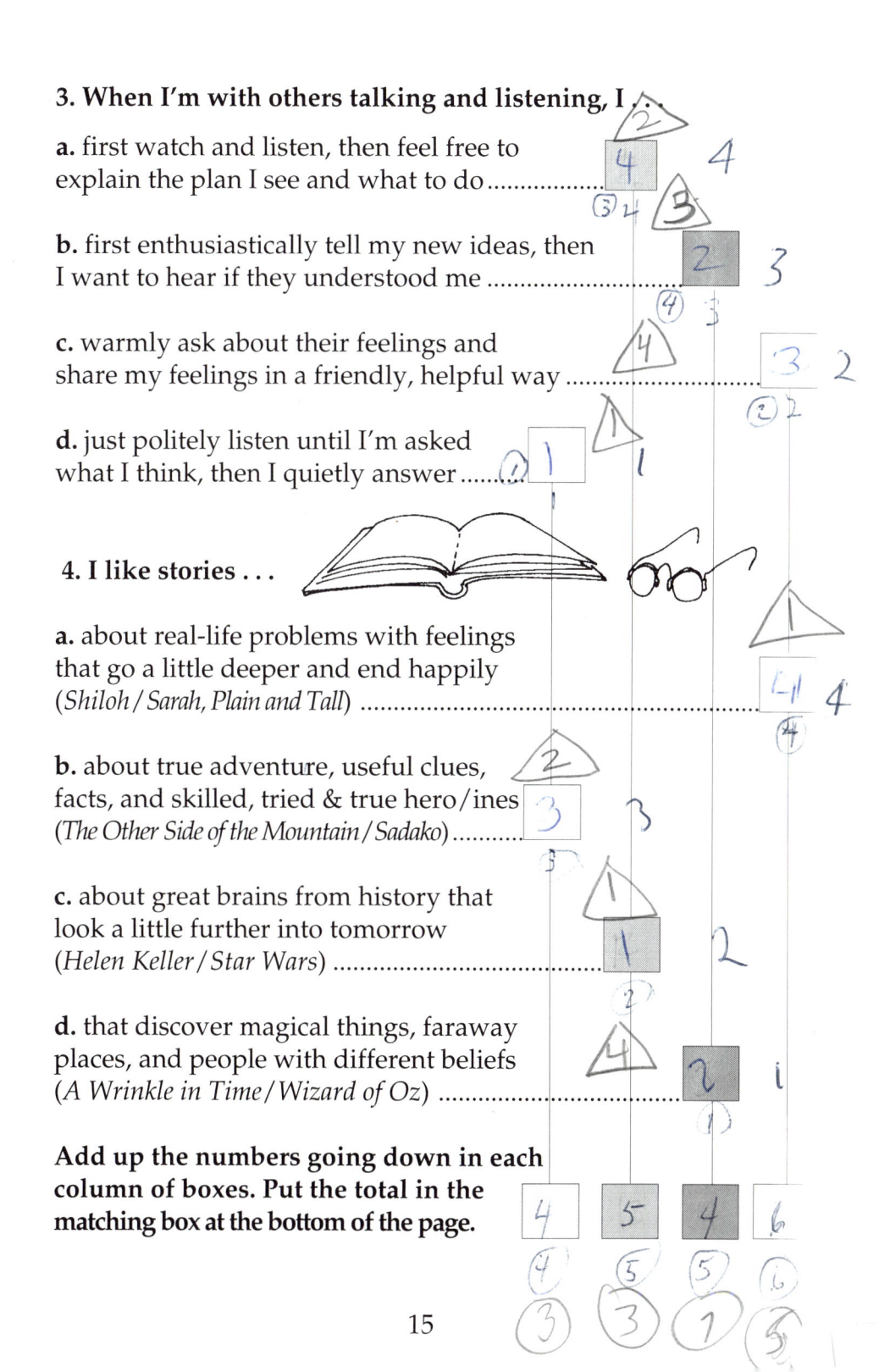

5. I solve my problems or make decisions best when . . .

a. I feel safe enough working with a group to ask other people to help me ....

b. I know the facts that tell me exactly what to do to get the right answer ....

c. I plan things my own way by comparing good and bad ideas to get quick results ....

d. I brainstorm with others, trust hunches, discover a new way to put ideas together ....

6. I like to play games that . . .

a. everyone has free-wheeling action and no one loses (playground merry-go-round) ....

b. have rules, lots of action to watch and someone wins (Monopoly/football) ....

c. allow me to direct, think or plan ahead (chess/follow-the-leader) ....

d. let me act things out or use my imagination (Pictionary/charades) ....

Add up the numbers going down in each column of boxes. Put the total in the matching box at the bottom of the page.

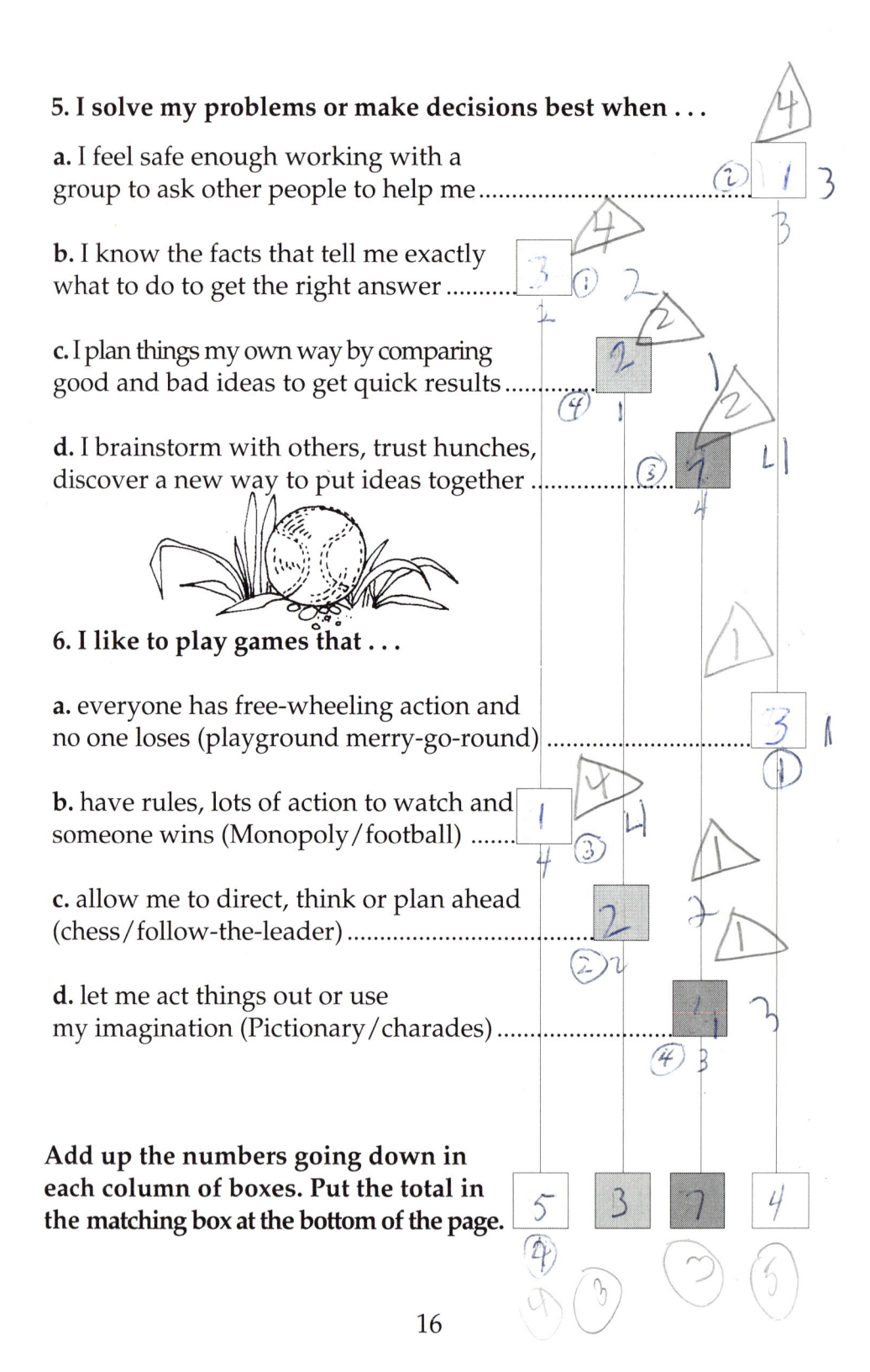

7. I learn best when . . .

a. I can bend the rules in a new way, discovering things out for myself ....

b. I can practice skills I already know while carefully following instructions ....

c. someone helps by showing me the easiest way to get things done ....

d. I can think ideas through, plan, set goals and get the job done on my own time ....

8. Sometimes, I don't want to . . .

a. risk a quarrel by telling the truth about how I feel, because if I hurt someone's feelings it takes **HARMONY** away ....

b. finish the things I start when I'm excited about something new, because I'll lose **UNDERSTANDING** of a new idea ....

c. be gentle and considerate of others' feelings because I'll lose the **FREEDOM** to get results based on my plan ....

d. make decisions when I don't know the facts, because I'll risk the **ORDER** I need to feel my world is a safe place .....

Add up the numbers going down in each column of boxes. Put the total in the matching box at the bottom of the page.

17

Now, let's add up the results.

First, add together the totals in each column on each of the four pages.
Enter the numbers in the boxes below.

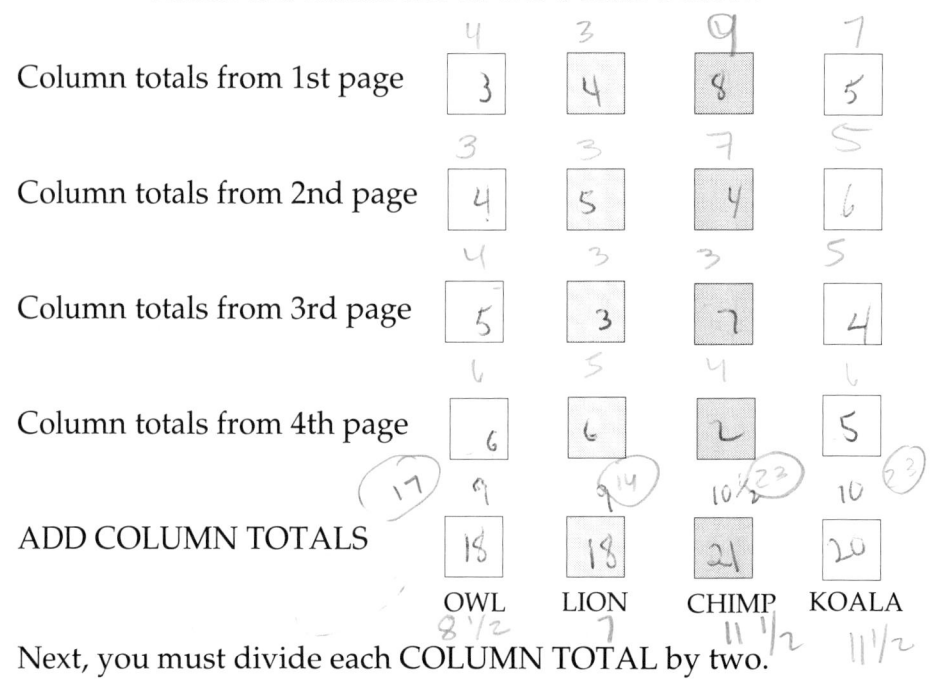

Column totals from 1st page: | 4 3 | 3 4 | 9 8 | 7 5 |

Column totals from 2nd page: | 3 4 | 3 5 | 7 4 | 5 6 |

Column totals from 3rd page: | 4 5 | 3 3 | 3 7 | 5 4 |

Column totals from 4th page: | 6 6 | 5 6 | 4 2 | 6 5 |

ADD COLUMN TOTALS: (17) 9 18 | 9 (14) 18 | 10 1/2 (22) 21 | 10 (23) 20

OWL   LION   CHIMP   KOALA
8 1/2   7   11 1/2   11 1/2

Next, you must divide each COLUMN TOTAL by two.

For example, if the total in the OWL box is 22, divide 22 by two which gives you a new total of 11. (22/2 = 11) If the total in the OWL box is 23, the new total would be 11 1/2. (Halves are okay!)

Think-about OWL total divided by 2	Look-about LION total divided by 2	Talk-about CHIMP total divided by 2	Feel-about KOALA total divided by 2
=	=	=	=

On the next page you'll find
the four animals around the growth rings of a tree.

Color in the same number of growth rings
as your final total for each animal.

For example:
If you have 11 as your final Owl total,
color 11 growth rings out from the center
of the tree trunk in the Owl section.

Color the rings of the Owl section grassy green. The orderly Think-about part of you is like grass, growing steadily and quietly.

Color the Lion section sky blue. The free-spirited Look-about part of you is like the cool, blue, open, visionary sky.

Color the Chimp section sunny yellow. The understanding, Talk-about part of you is like the bright light of the energizing sun.

Color the Koala section earthy red. The harmonious Feel-about part of you is like the warm, comforting, friendly earth.

This is the center core of your wholehearted feelings and deeply rooted values of well-being.

Your Heart-wood Center

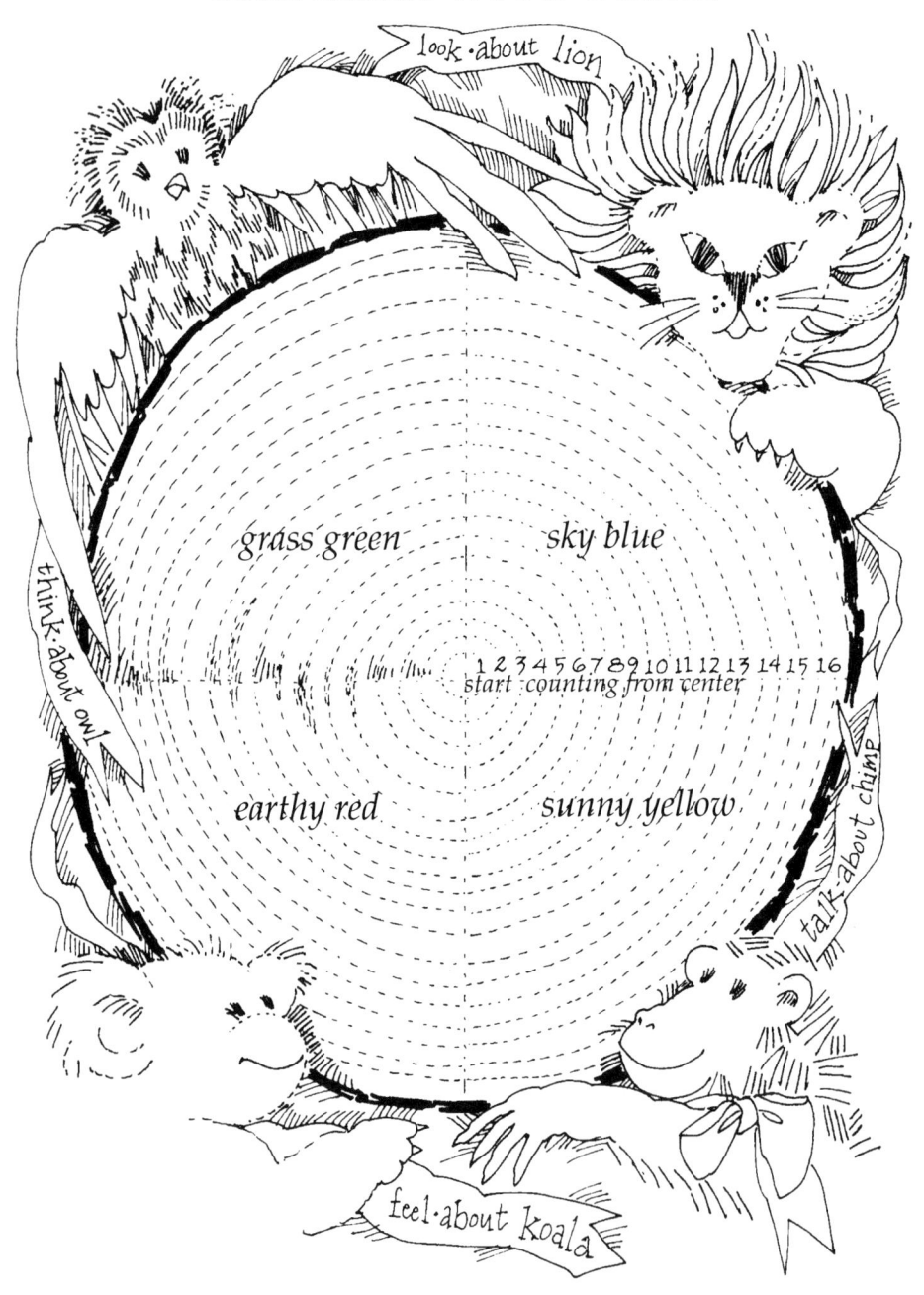

look·about lion

think·about owl

grass green *sky blue*

1 2 3 4 5 6 7 8 9 10 11 12 13 14 15 16
start counting from center

earthy red *sunny yellow*

talk·about chimp

feel·about koala

Color from the inside out just the way the tree grows from its heart.

Look at the section where you colored the most rings.
This is your special Inside self.

Think-about Owl   **Look-about Lion**

If you have more Owl rings, you prefer to think about facts and put things in order. You work toward perfection and want the world to be a safe place. You have difficulty expressing your fears, feelings and opinions.

If you have more Lion rings, you prefer to look about at surroundings and see how everything could be made better. You prefer to focus on a plan, rather than a feeling. You like to take charge and get results.

If you have more Koala rings, you prefer to trust your feelings. You are quiet, friendly, and helpful. You like peaceful moments, to feel you belong, and to make things. You have difficulty expressing fear, anger and worry, holding them inside.

If you have more Chimp rings, you prefer to talk about ideas first and get reactions. You like to hear how ideas sound. You express excitement, anger and love, and want understanding. You like everyone to have fun talking together.

Feel-about Koala   **Talk-about Chimp**

This is a very brief look at the four different kinds of people; the center core of your feelings and deeply rooted values show you what your natural talents are!

The Koala and Chimp are more spatial and prefer to feel more than to think. The reasonable Owl and Lion prefer to think. The Owl and Koala are slower to decide, until the idea catches in their mind. They learn by doing hands-on things, while the Lion and the Chimp make up their minds quickly, learning to ponder the big picture.

Look again at the growth rings you colored. Is one section larger and stronger than the others? Or, are they all about the same?

If you are like most people, you have two sections that are stronger. It's important to have strong natural talents which you can recognize and rely on.

Really strong natural talents also mean you have other talents which you rarely use and may have difficulty understanding, especially in other people.

On the next page, OUTLINE THE LARGE SQUARE with green, blue, yellow or red. If your largest growth ring is blue, outline the Look-about square. Then INSIDE this blue square, OUTLINE THE LITTLE SQUARE which shows you your second largest growth ring. If your second largest ring is yellow, outline the small Talk-about square INSIDE the large Look-about square.

Learn to Use Your Less-Preferred Talents

Skill Master
Think-about talents

Vision Leader
Look-about talents

Librarian	Detective	Lawyer	Architect
\multicolumn{2}{l	}{Needs to serve}	\multicolumn{2}{l}{Need expert knowledge}
\multicolumn{2}{l	}{Careful about time & facts}	\multicolumn{2}{l}{Use best facts and ideas}
\multicolumn{2}{l	}{Self-assured and detailed}	\multicolumn{2}{l}{PURPOSEful problem solving}
\multicolumn{2}{l	}{Knows PATTERNS in things}	\multicolumn{2}{l}{Practical results & choices}
\multicolumn{2}{c	}{*Root Value*}	\multicolumn{2}{c}{*Root Value*}
\multicolumn{2}{c	}{*Order*}	\multicolumn{2}{c}{*Freedom*}
Engineer	News Reporter	Farmer	Inventor
Craftsman	Fireman	Entrepreneur	Professor
\multicolumn{2}{c	}{*Root Value*}	\multicolumn{2}{c}{*Root Value*}
\multicolumn{2}{c	}{*Harmony*}	\multicolumn{2}{c}{*Understanding*}
Musician	Actor	Pioneer	Sales
\multicolumn{2}{l	}{Need hands-on action}	\multicolumn{2}{l}{Need inspired ideas}
\multicolumn{2}{l	}{Trust your RANDOM feelings}	\multicolumn{2}{l}{Trust your future dreams}
\multicolumn{2}{l	}{listen to your body}	\multicolumn{2}{l}{Time to listen & talk}
\multicolumn{2}{l	}{Spend time with friends & crafts}	\multicolumn{2}{l}{Risk a CHANCE idea}

Peace Maker
Feel-about talents

Dream Mover
Talk-about talents

Remember our discussion of Inner Maps?

It may seem nice to have a clear path to follow, but clear, well-used paths mean there is much we never explore. There may even be fences to keep you from traveling beyond your usual path.

We need to *think*, *see*, *hear* and *feel* all our natural talents, both *inside* and *outside*, so our growth is balanced and our own tree of life grows straight and tall.

The chart on the next page compares our root values and natural talents. It's natural for us to favor one or two talents over others. Notice how the Owl and the Lion prefer *thinking* over *feeling* while the Koala and Chimp prefer *feeling* over *thinking*.

The Owl and Koala are like each other, because they prefer to work on things in an inside-sort-of-way. The Lion and Chimp are just the opposite. They prefer to express themselves by doing things in an outside-sort-of-way.

The way we CHANGE something in our world, depends on which talents we favor and which things we PAY ATTENTION to going on around us. Changing your mind changes your inner world.

Think-about Owl   Look-about Lion

Serves Others Cool colors Neat/neat **Order** **Facts** *Prefers* **Safety** *Thinking* Thinks things over Takes time making decisions Asks questions and listens Watches others	Knowledge Cool colors Neat/messy **Freedom** **Choices** **Results** Takes risks Makes decisions quickly Answers questions and talks Expresses to others
Action Warm colors Messy/neat **Harmony** **Belonging** *Prefers* **Hands-on** *Feeling* Thinks things over Takes time making decisions Asks questions and listens Watches others	Creativity Warm colors Messy/messy **Understanding** **Ideas** **Creativity** Takes risks Quickly makes decisions Answers questions and talks Expresses to others

Feel-about Koala   Talk-about Chimp

On this page, outline the large square
with your animal's colors,
green, blue, yellow or red.
If your largest growth ring is blue,
outline the Look-about square.

a logical grass green think about owl

feel about koala

an earthy feeling red

look·about lion

a visionary blue

talk·about·chimp

a sunny idea yellow

0 1 2 3 4 5 6 7 8 9 10 11 12 13 14 15 16

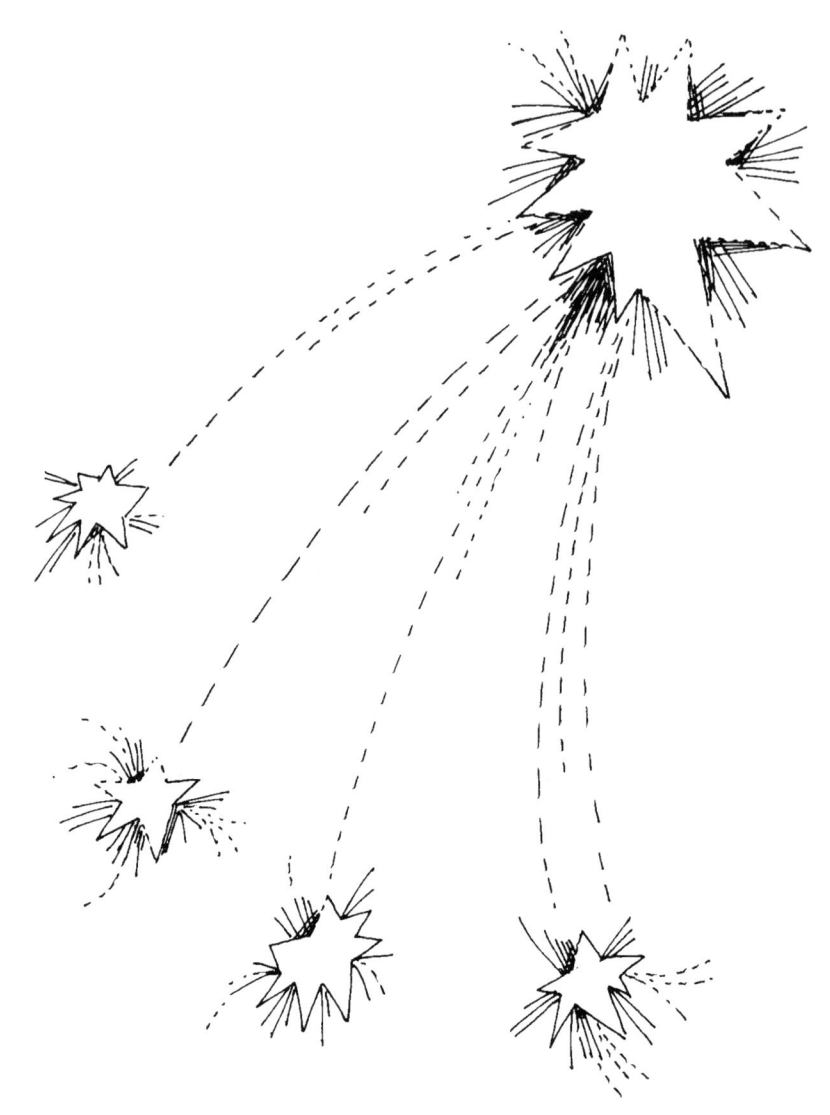

"The trees in the street are old trees used to living with people, family trees that remember your grandfather's name."

A Child

Just Like a Tree

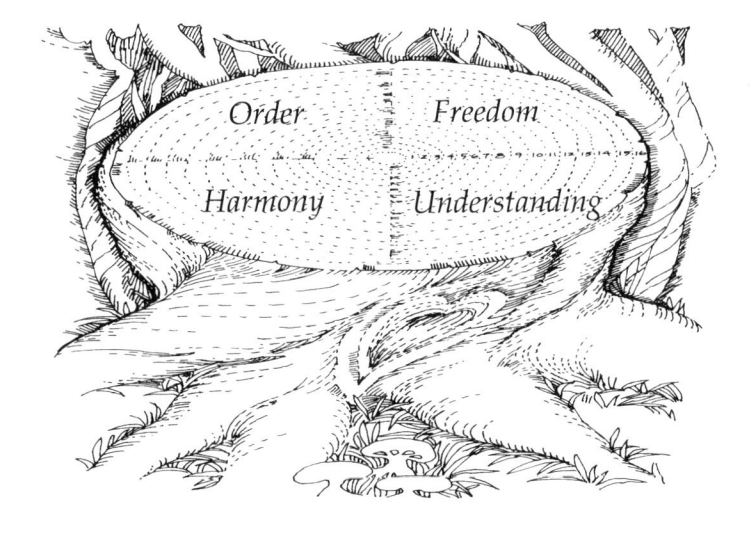

We all need strong roots and good support to stretch and grow. Our strong roots come from our values — what matters to us most. Each of us experiences life differently and therefore writes a different story. But what is common to us all is learning how to make new meanings out of good and bad moments. When we do this, we learn to stretch and grow on the Inside and work and belong together on the Outside, uncovering our own true roots.

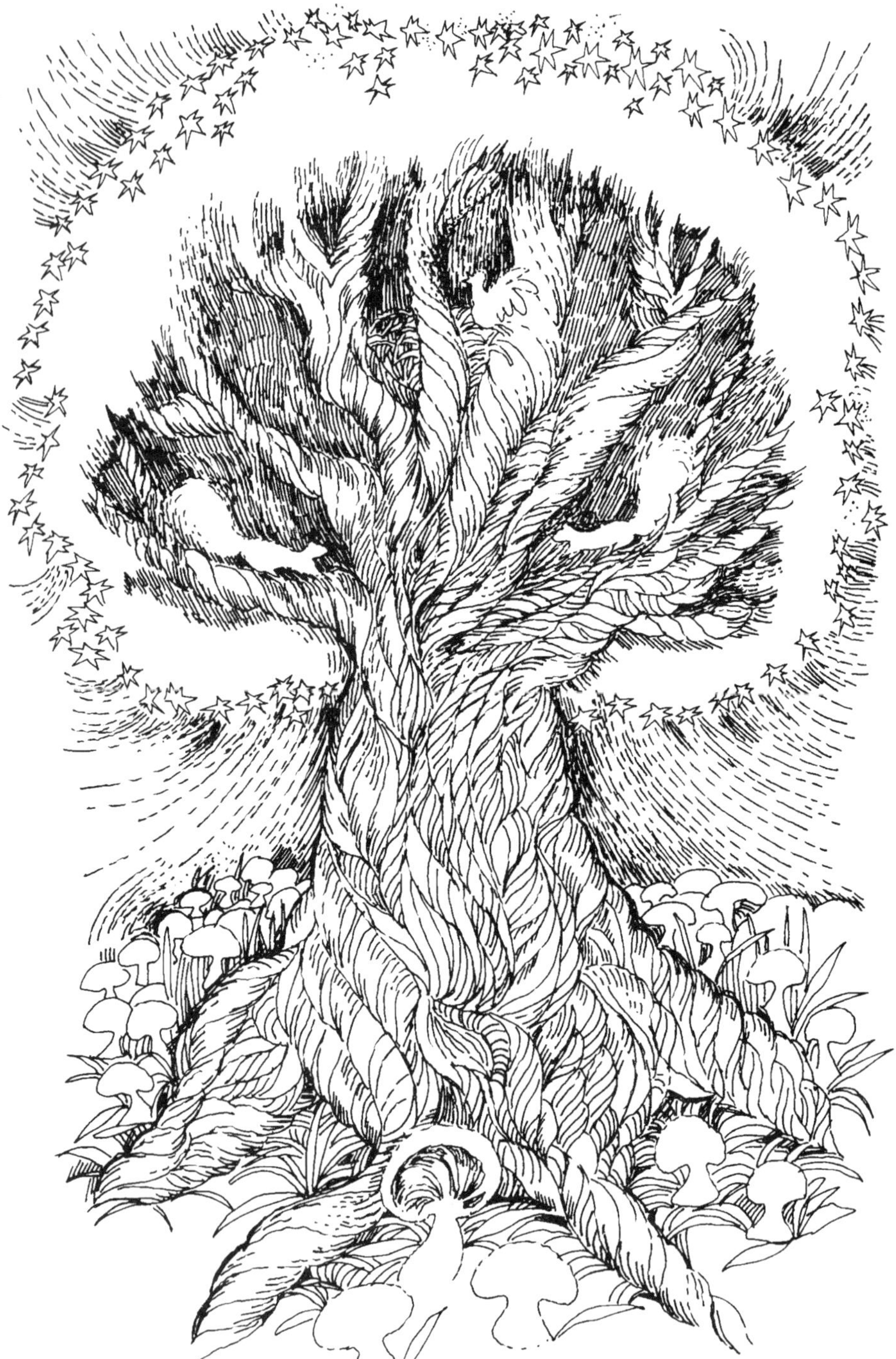

The Think-about Person

Owls are left-brained and love to serve people. They prefer facts more than hunches. They are called *organized* people, because they take the logical approach to things. Sometimes Owls prefer grey or other light, soft, natural colors.

The Owl is the Skill Master

Owls take things in as information, rules, data, past experiences. Owls are comfortable asking questions, listening and watching others. Owls prefer to gather information and think about it in careful, factual ways. They find patterns in nature and things to help them create order. That's why Owls are neat/neat people who put everything back in the right place. Owls need time to think things over and make decisions. They work to keep the world a safe place where things will stay the same because they see the natural patterns in nature. ***They always see the risks of change; that's why their glass is half empty.*** They ask, "What's missing in this Idea?" They like things done the right way. They do have feelings and fears, though they rarely put them in words. They are stressed when there is no order or stability. They can become negative, unfriendly and stubborn in order to get their right way.

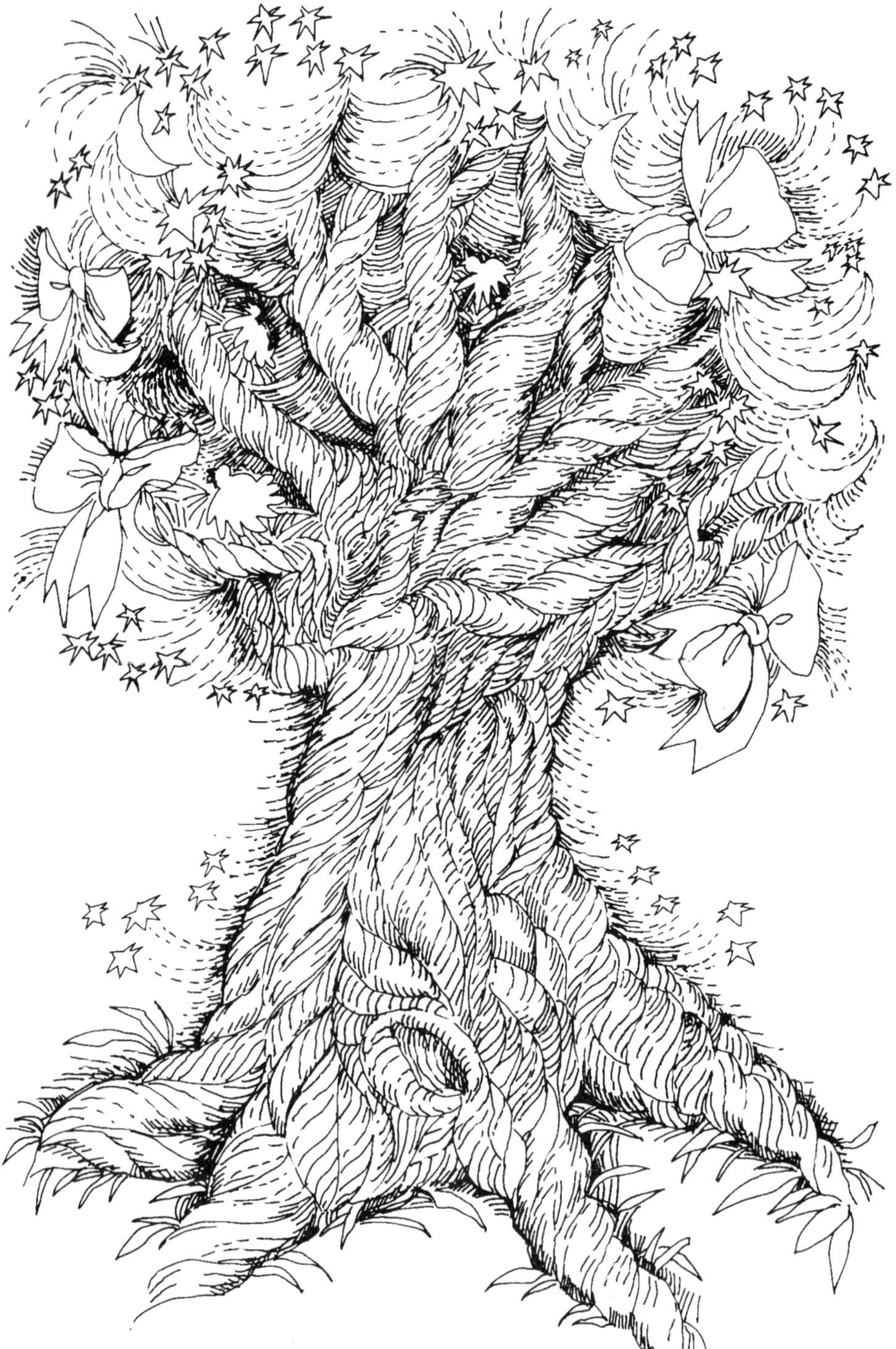

The Look-about Person

Lions are left-brained. They love knowledge. They prefer to think more than feel. They are called *visual* people, because they prefer to look about at their surroundings and picture things in their minds. Lions prefer bold, darker-toned natural colors.

The Lion is the Vision Leader

Lions put things into action — plans, leadership, authority, results. Lions are comfortable answering questions, talking and expressing themselves. Lions see how everything could be made better. They like to do things their own way. They can envision a plan and are very convincing when they explain the plan. ***They take control of the best ideas and facts and get results. That is why Lions own the glass.*** They like to get to the point; they are willing to take risks and make decisions quickly. Lions are both neat/messy people. They keep a lot of things stuffed in the drawers. They take charge, involve others and get results. Lions get stressed when they lose choices, vision or independence. They can be hostile, bossy and they may yell in order to get their own way.

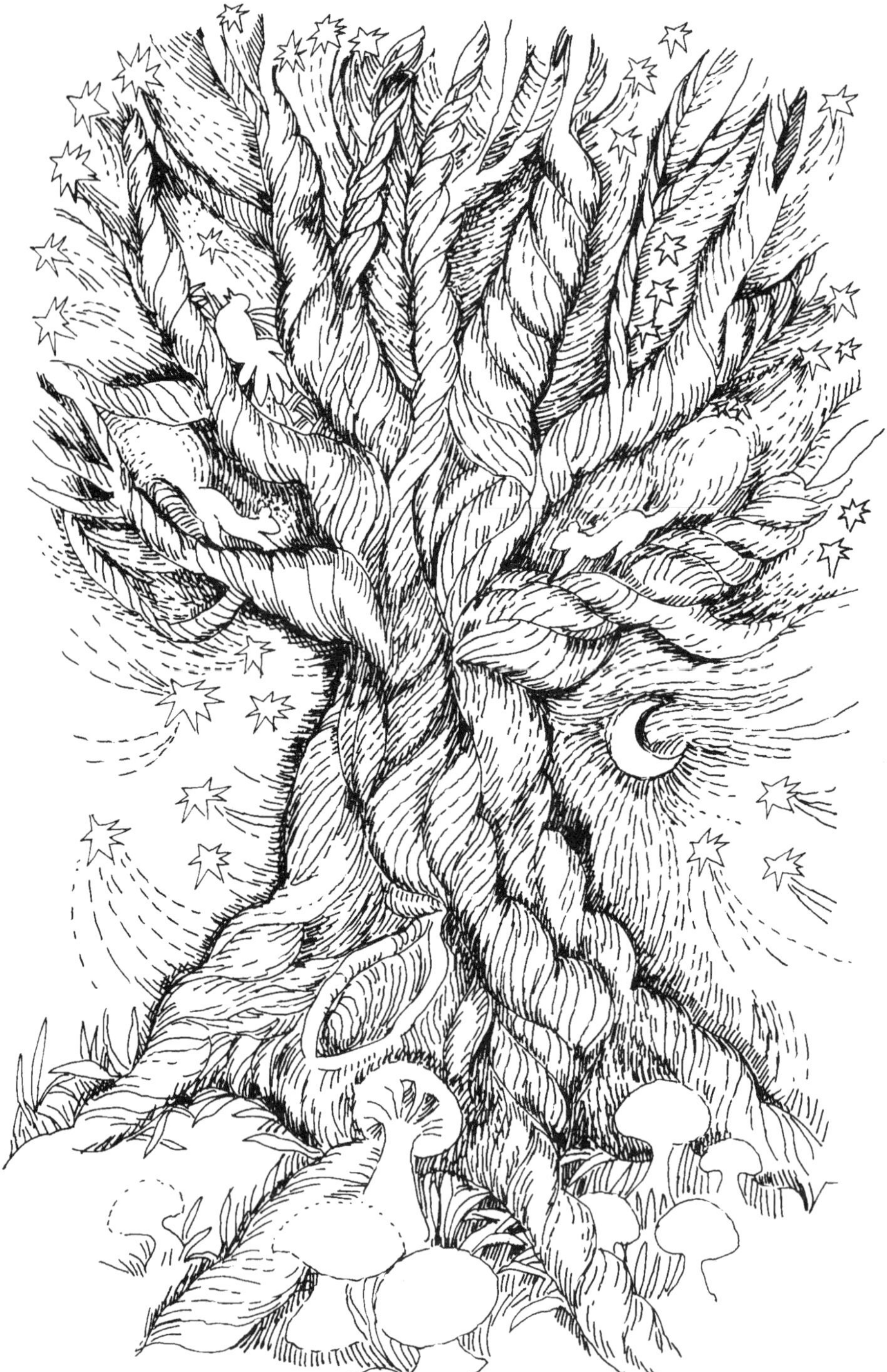

The Talk-about Person

Chimps are right-brained and love new ideas. They prefer hunches more than logic. They are called *auditory* people because they respond to the tone of voice and like to hear how ideas sound. They like warm, bright colors and bold combinations.

The Chimp is the Dream Mover

Chimps put things into communication — ideas, creations, inspirations, questions. Chimps like to talk about their ideas, so others will respond. They love to be inspired. Chimps like to learn on their own, question the rules, take risks and try new things. Chimps are messy/messy people. They file by pile. They want to be understood and to understand why people believe and act as they do. They are creative problem-solvers; they like to do things a new way. ***They look on the bright side, that is why their glass is half full (not half empty).*** When Chimps are excited, angry or loving, everyone within earshot knows. Chimps get stressed when they feel they're not understood. They can be resentful, worried, depressed.

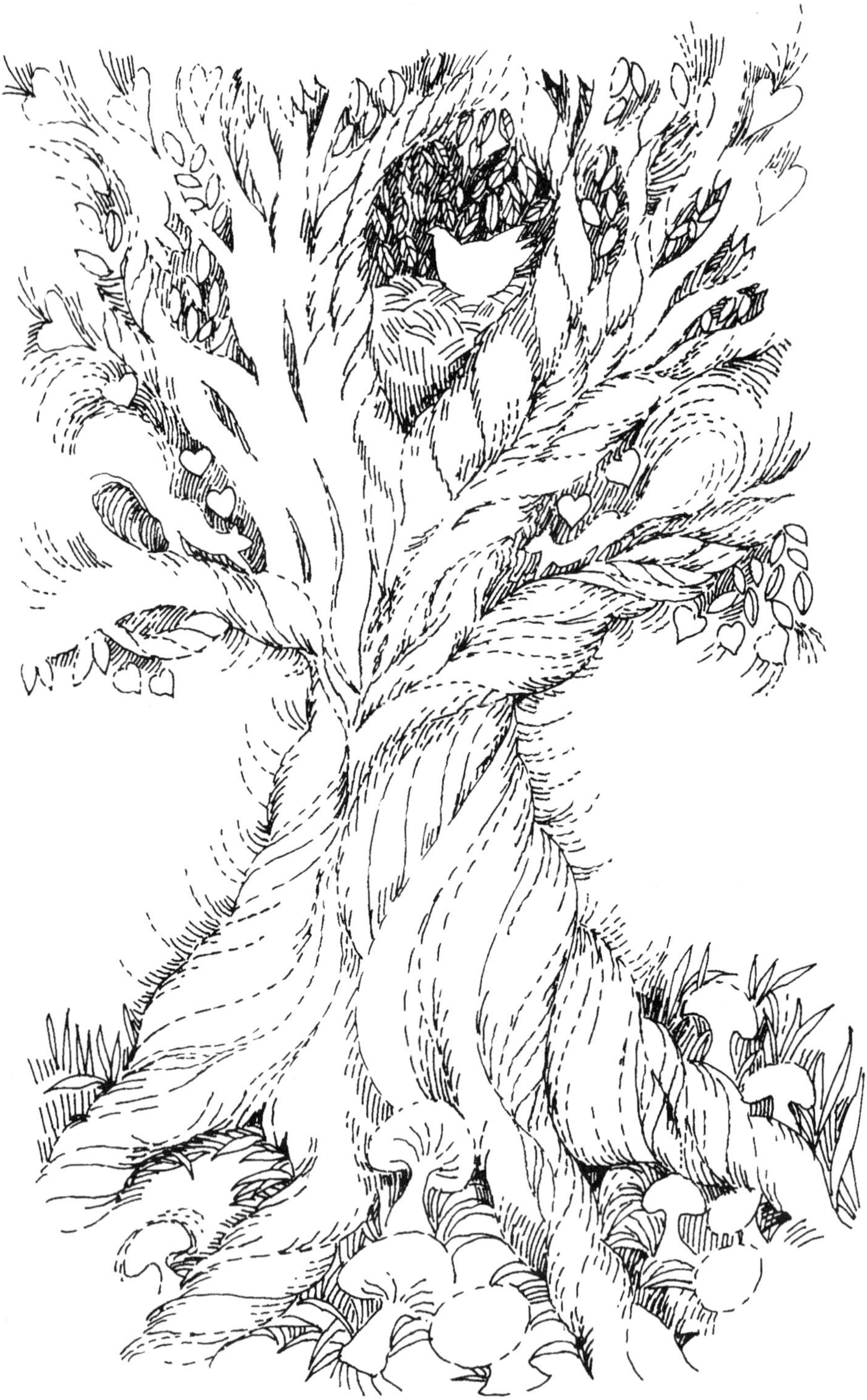

The Feel-about Person

Koalas are right-brained and love action. They prefer to feel more than think. They are called *kinesthetic* people, which means they are sensitive to how their emotions and body feel. They prefer warm, soft, quiet, pastel colors.

The Koala is the Peace Maker

Koalas understand such things as feelings — emotions, movement, impressions. They are quiet, friendly people good at coordinating gatherings because they are cheerful and like to do things in a happy way. Koalas are adaptive and flexible; they don't like to disagree *because they feel caught in the middle of both sides. That's why their glass is both half-full and half-empty.* They want to know the concerns of the group, they want to be helpful and a part of things. Koalas learn by doing and are clever at making things by hand. They like to make things up as they go. Koalas are messy/neat people who save things with old memories. They may hold anger and worries Inside, rather than risk a quarrel or talking back. They get stressed when there is a loss of *harmony* or belonging. They can be whiny, gossipy or sneaky in order to get their own way.

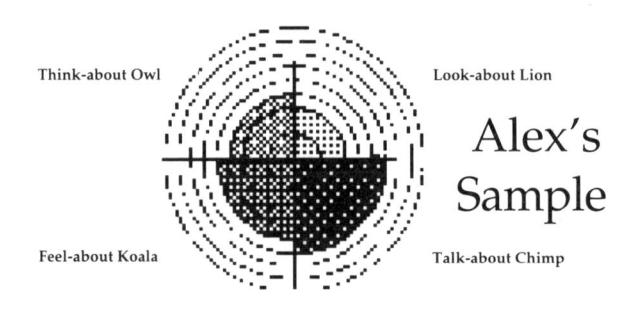

Think-about Owl

Look-about Lion

Alex's Sample

Feel-about Koala

Talk-about Chimp

Uu is for us

Alex 1970
Xx is for Xtra love

The Center Cores of Your Family Tree

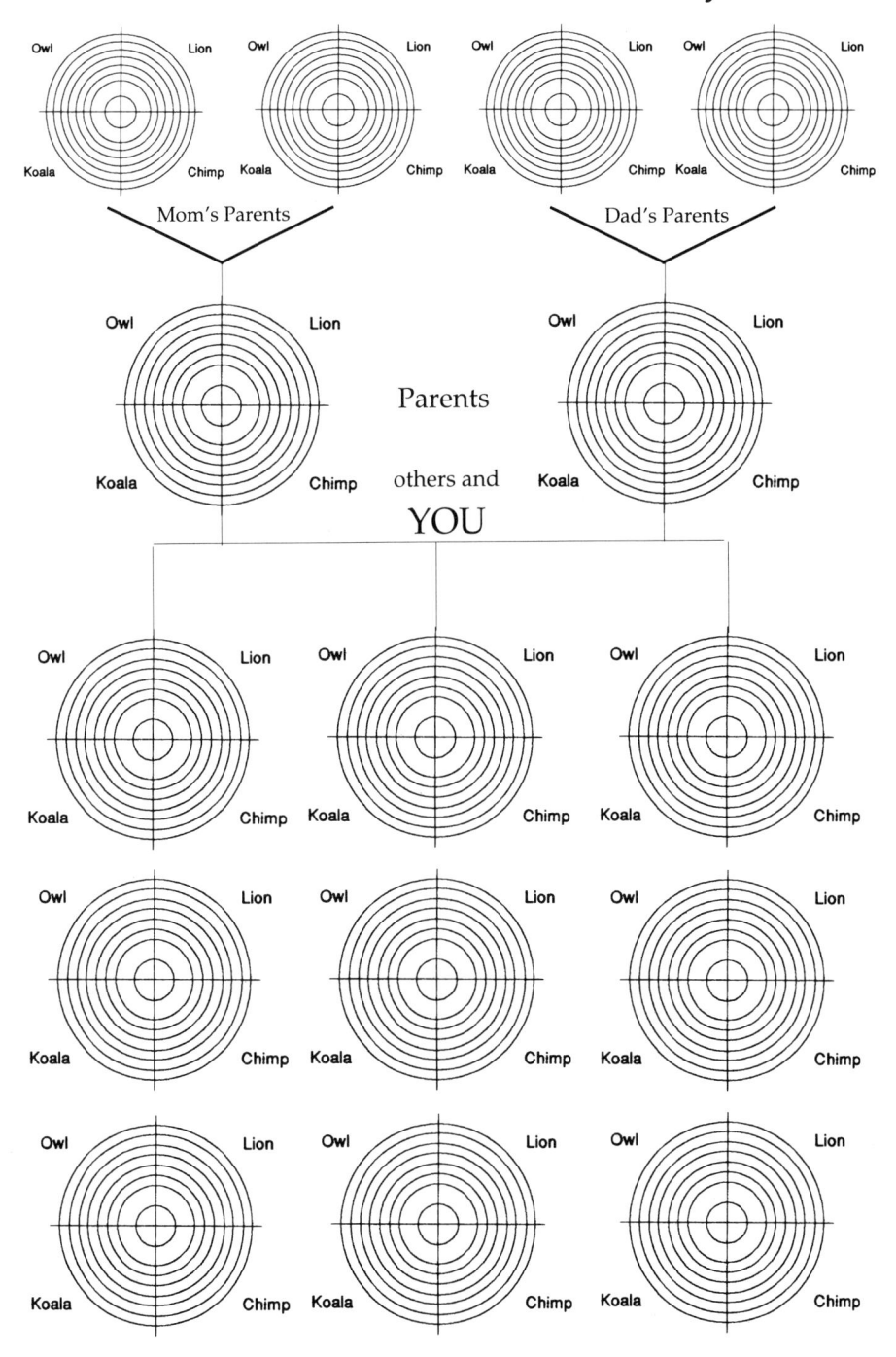

Mom's Parents

Dad's Parents

Parents

others and
YOU

On the opposite page you are looking down at the top of a tree, which is its growing edge. Its growing from the four root values stretching from without and compressing within its trunk, your emotional core.

Find your root value and put your name in the leaves growing there. Next, think about the people you live with — your family, friends, etc. Put each one's name in a group of leaves growing from the root value — **order, freedom, understanding** and **harmony** you — think is the most real and true for them.

Next draw branches to connect you with each of them. Draw strong branches to the people you feel close to — those who listen and understand you the most. Draw thinner branches to those who don't know you very well. Draw broken branches to those with whom you have troubles.

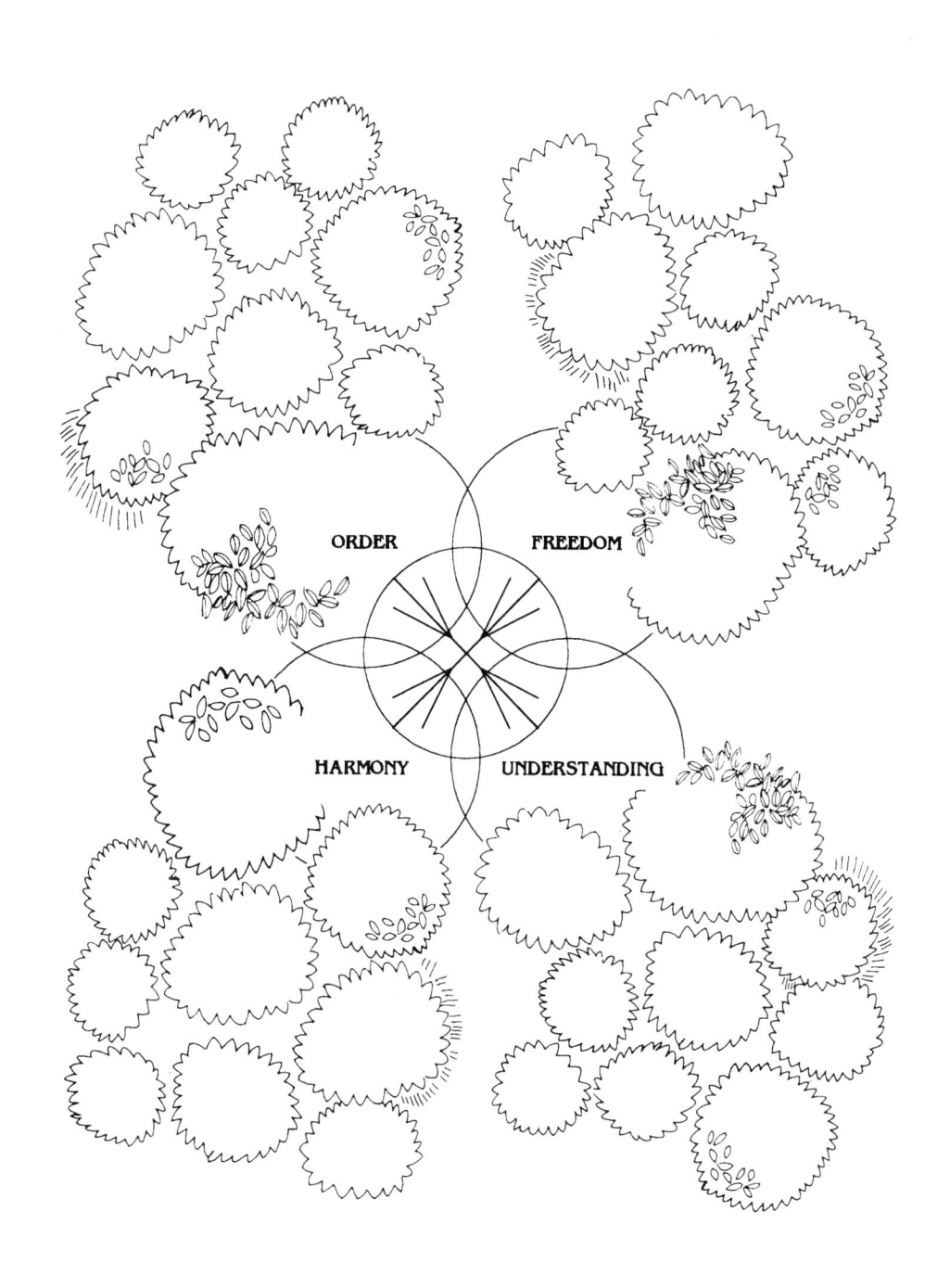

ORDER　　FREEDOM

HARMONY　　UNDERSTANDING

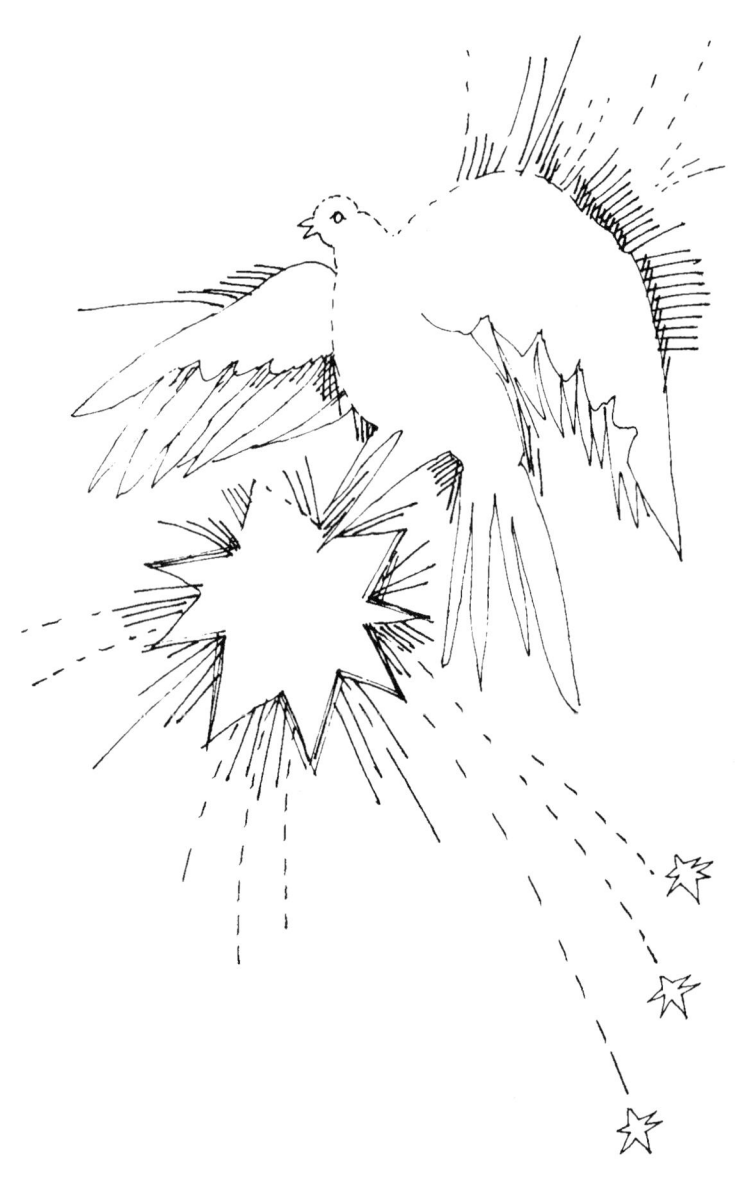

"*Birds build their nests in circles for theirs is the same religion as ours.*"
Black Elk

The Think-about Owl Finds Order

When I'm a Think-about Owl

If I were an Owl, a Think-about Owl,
you'd find me alone in my room
enjoying the quiet, enjoying my thoughts,
so don't interrupt me too soon.

Oh, I love to ponder the meaning
and wonder
the workings of this and of that . . .
the order of numbers and
patterns and rhythms
of systems and logic and maps.

I like my room neat and it's really a treat
for me to arrange it my way,
so don't wait around for a finishing sound,
I just might be busy all day.

I'd be amazed to see on paper all the figuring and all the feelings going through my mind in one day.

I need things in order and
a predictable future
with everything tidy and straight.
If things get too messy
or plans get too iffy,
how can I expect to create?

When I am aware of confusion
and scared,
I freeze and don't know
what to do.
Then I can get stubborn,
unfriendly and snappy
and even
stop talking to you.

*It's okay for me to like details and
want things in order.*

Now please understand
that I do need a friend,
and my feelings don't know what to say.
You'll just have to know
I like you although
I seem to be running away.

I really like facts and
step-by-step explanations,
then I work the best that I can.
So, tell me exactly just what you expect
then I'll know what ideas you plan.

Just give me some time for being alone
to get my surroundings to mend.
Then I'll be ready for more conversations
and riddles and games with my friend.

When I feel safe, it's easy for me to work and have fun with other people who are very different from me.

Think-about Owl

Your head listens to your heart and finds order

I need to feel everything is in order, safe and correct! When I'm a Think-about kind of person, I like to . . .
(check the boxes which are most like you)

- ☐ take my time before I act on an idea.
- ☐ use skills I already have.
- ☐ explain ideas step-by-step.
- ☐ earn my own spending money.
- ☐ read about how things are discovered and the reasons why they are special.
- ☐ control my own things and have a special place where I make the rules.
- ☐ see the patterns in things with lists, maps, directions or signs that tell me which way to go.
- ☐ keep my ideas to myself until I'm ready to speak.

☐ know exactly what to do.
☐ have all my things lined up in order.
☐ not have to tell others how I really feel, if I'm upset.
☐ be on time and have my friends be on time to meet me.
☐ be loyal to my friends and take good care of my pets.

Think-about You

What's going through
my mind today?

What sort of things
do I most like
to keep in order?

Who do I feel safe with
and like to do things with?

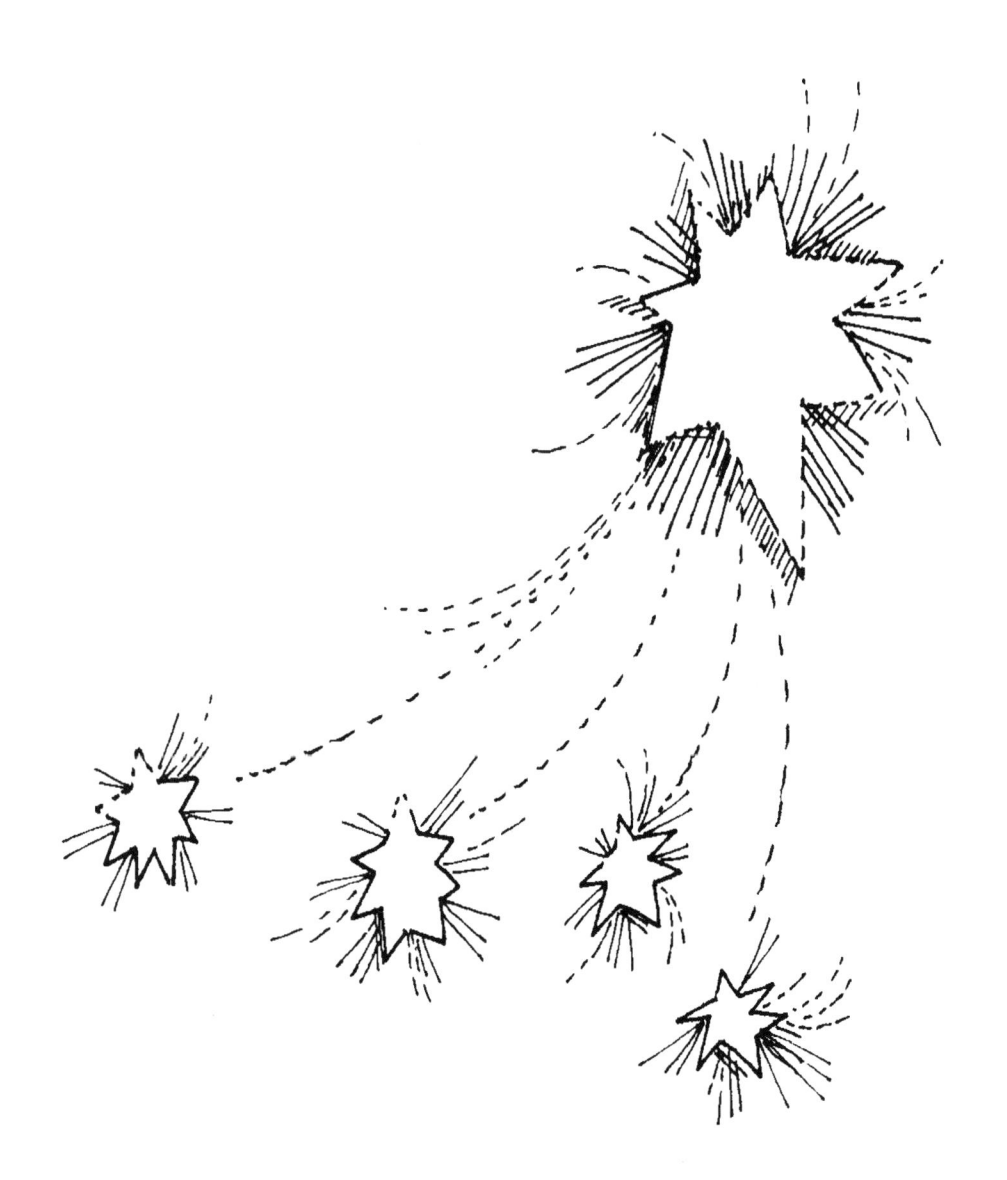

"A fellow can't think or feel accurately unless he knows something."
Mark Twain

The Look-about Lion

Shapes Freedom

When I'm a Look-about Lion

If I were a Lion, a Look-about Lion,
the world would be mine to explore.
I'd be a leader or a new-thing inventor,
to do what's never been tried yet before.

My plans are so huge,
so tall and so wide
they go far into reaches of space.
I wish to move forward
and upward and onward
and follow my vision someplace.

I'm a person of action.
I see the attraction
of having control of my fate.
I like to take charge of projects so large,
and, with others, accomplish the great.

I know I could build wonderful things — houses, boats and giant rockets to explore outer space.

So don't get in my way
or interfere day-to-day
with the task
I've set for myself.
For I must be free
to do wondrous deeds;
not tied up or put on the shelf.

And if I feel caged,
I'll roar and I'll rage,
I'll yell,
I'll demand
and I'll snap.
I'll quickly take action
in any direction
that might get me out of a trap.

*I'm brave and always ready to explore.
I can see in my mind a plan that will get things done.*

I always need freedom
and room to move on.
I hate things that get in my way.
You may feel amazed,
confronted and dazed
or hurt by the things that I say.

Please understand
that's the way that I am —
the way that I try to break free.
Don't cower or cringe
if your feelings get singed,
just stand up and tell it to me.

I feel good when everyone cooperates in one of my projects, and I feel proud when I can take charge to make sure the job is done well.

Look-about Lion

**I need to feel free, have choices and get results!
When I'm a Look-about kind of person, I like to . . .**

- [ ] imagine what life will be like in the future.
- [ ] choose by myself the direction I want to go.
- [ ] search for solutions to problems.
- [ ] work on something that takes a long time.
- [ ] have a quiet place where I can think.
- [ ] watch somebody work while they explain to me what they're doing.
- [ ] choose clothes that are my favorite colors and make me look good.
- [ ] look at pictures in books and read stories that explain the how and why of things.

- ☐ draw diagrams to explain my ideas.
- ☐ see by their smiling face that someone likes me.
- ☐ have lots of pencils, colored markers and big sheets of clean paper for me to use.
- ☐ to talk or listen only when I want to.
- ☐ have the colors and things around me look nice and neat.
- ☐ go to museums or other interesting places and explore them for as long as I want.

Look-about you

What would I invent and what places would I explore?

What plans or projects do I have now?

What projects have I done well with others?

> "I know but one freedom,
> and that is the freedom of the mind."
> Antoine de Saint Exupery

The Talk-about Chimp

Seeks Understanding

When I'm a Talk-about Chimp

If I were a Chimp, a Talk-about Chimp,
ideas would whirl through my mind.
They'd dance 'til I'm crazy and
twirl 'til I'm dizzy,
until I can barely unwind.

I'm good at pretending,
expressing, inventing,
I'm artist and actor at play.
I'm often creative and so innovative,
I do everything in a new way.

I like to be out with nature about.
There's so much to hear 'neath the sky.
A talk with my friend is the very best way
to catch the ideas that fly by.

*I love to talk to friends about ideas,
and I have so very many questions.*

I crave understanding.
I can be demanding
with wishes not easily met.
With your indecision or even derision,
I'll frown and I'll fidget and fret.

If you reject me, it hurts.
Ignoring's the worst
I ever have to endure.
Then I put off things,
withdraw, become moody,
depressed and completely unsure.

*I love it when I can
do something new and different.*

I love to question the rules
and the reasons
and do what seems right to me.
I need your affection and
true understanding
to feel that I really am free.

So, give me a hand;
please listen and lend
your thoughts to the project I've planned.
For I need to know,
that I can be friends
with someone who does understand.

*When I can have fun with friends
creating and performing a show, I feel great!*

Talk-about Chimp

**I need to understand and be understood and to share my ideas and be creative.
When I'm a Talk-about kind of person, I . . .**

- [ ] hear people explain how to do something.
- [ ] choose what I want to learn.
- [ ] shout with joy.
- [ ] find different ways to do an assignment.
- [ ] hear people talking in soft, nice voices all around me.
- [ ] talk to myself while I do a problem or task.
- [ ] talk about what scares me or what makes me angry or happy.

- ☐ talk in a loud or quiet voice,
  whichever sounds good to me.
- ☐ hear about legends and myths
  and what other people believe.
- ☐ talk when everyone is listening, share
  my ideas first, and see how others react.
- ☐ play games that use my
  ideas and imagination.
- ☐ do lots of different things at the same time.
- ☐ be in plays where I can talk.

Talk-about You

Who listens to and
understands me?

What questions
are on my mind today?

If I were going to do
a show,
what kind of a
show would it be?

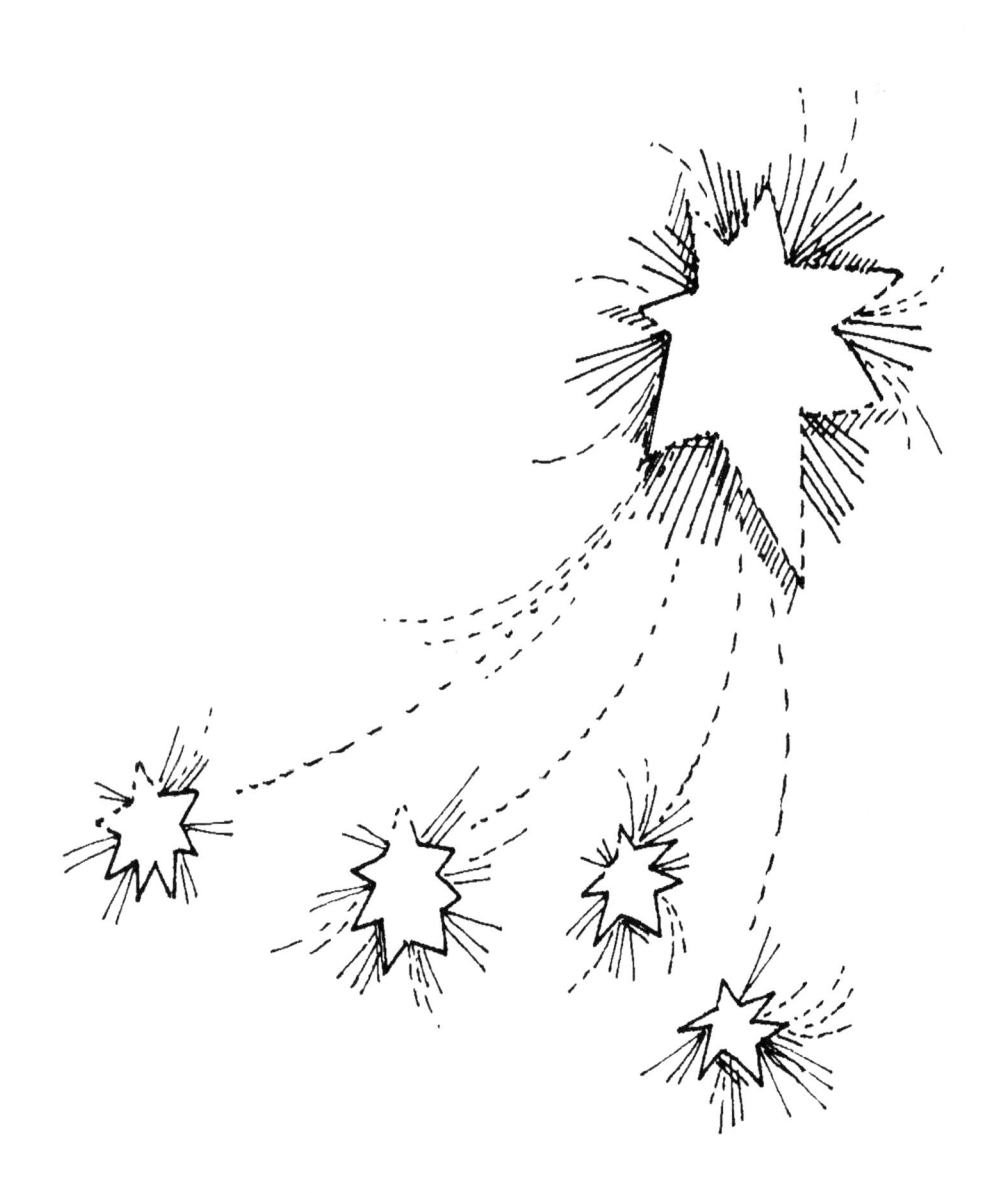

"*All my life
I've had an awareness
of other times and places.*"
                    Jack London

The Feel-about Koala

Loves Harmony

When I'm a Feel-about Koala

If I were a Koala, a Feel-about Koala,
you'd find me surrounded by friends.
For I love to chatter with people
who matter.
I hope that the fun never ends.

I help all my friends to get along well
and help them be part of a team.
With everyone working
and playing together,
I'm flexible, smiling, serene.

My favorite place to sit is the sofa
surrounded by pillows and rugs.
I'd like to feed everyone
cookies and cocoa,
cheerfully giving them hugs.

*I love to do nice things for my friends,
especially make gifts for them.*

But tell me you're angry, bluster and yell,
and you'll find me shrinking away.
Don't make me feel silly
and shove me around
or I'll struggle to get my own way.

For I can be snappy, whiny and prickly,
when I am feeling left out.
To get me involved
in a plan with my friends,
believe me;
you don't have to shout.

*I love to sit in a cozy chair and daydream
about happy people helping each other.*

Just give me a part
to play in each game
with everyone getting along.
A crowd where people
are working together
will help me to feel I belong.

I love to have harmony,
smiling and sweet,
whenever I'm part of the plan.
And I need the compliments
coming from you
to make me feel
precious and grand.

*I love parties and celebrations where
I can listen to the gentle laughter of my friends
while we all eat together.*

Feel-about Koala

**I need to feel in harmony with everything around me, that my feelings matter and I belong.
When I'm a Feel-about kind of person, I like to . . .**

- ☐ learn by doing and making things with my hands.
- ☐ hug and be hugged by people I like.
- ☐ have noisy fun.
- ☐ know everybody is friends with me.
- ☐ dance all around to music.
- ☐ ride my bike fast and feel the wind on my face and the motions in my body.
- ☐ wear clothes that are neat, but it's okay for me to get them dirty or rumpled.
- ☐ listen only as long as I want to.

- [ ] sit in any chair I want, whenever I want.
- [ ] feel it's okay to let everyone know how I feel.
- [ ] work on something right away and think about what I'm doing as I go along.
- [ ] not have to pay attention to the clock.

Feel-about You

What sort of things do I like to make with my hands?

Whom have I helped that appreciated what I did?

Who are the people I like to be together with?

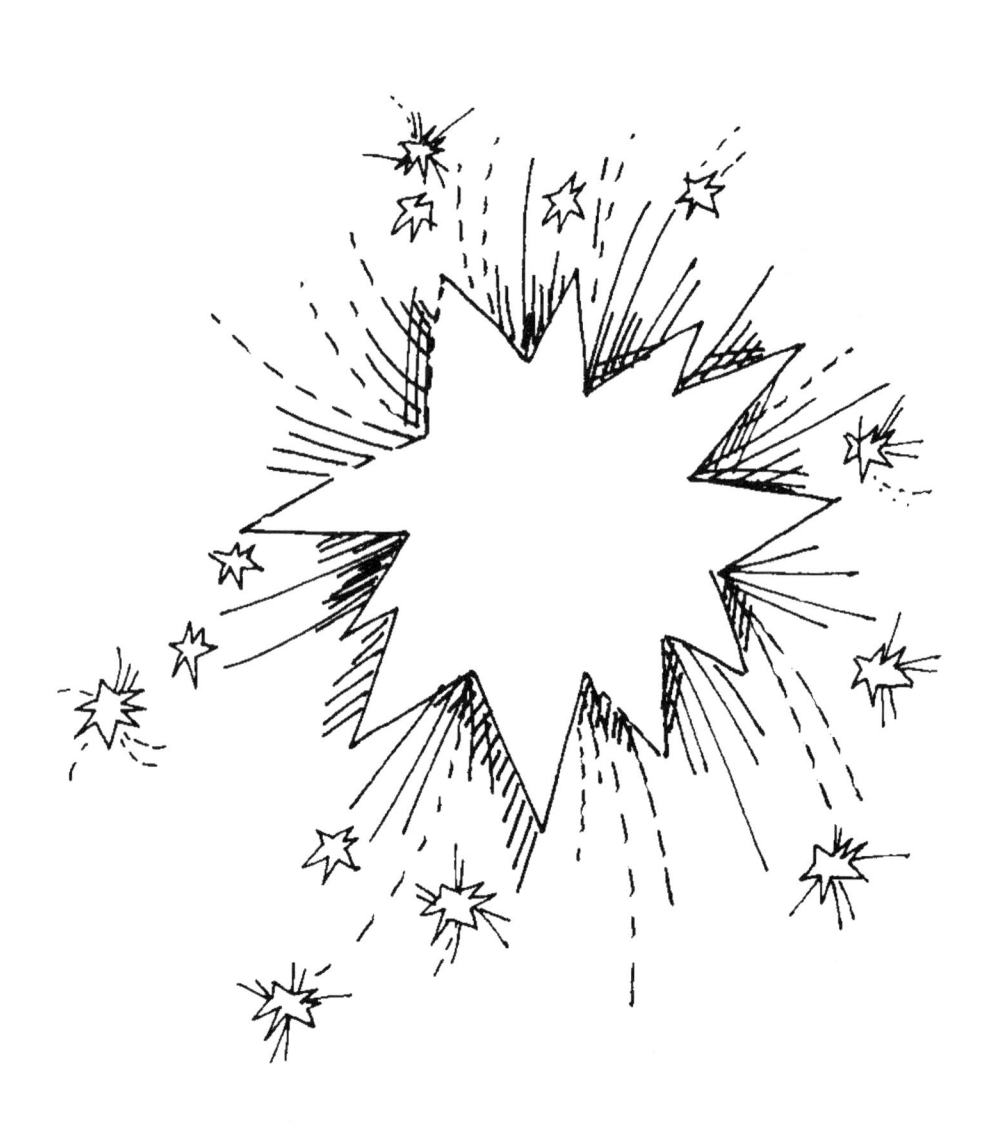

"*The whole purpose of Art and Science is to awaken the cosmic religious feeling.*"
Albert Einstein

Discover Your Deeply-rooted Values

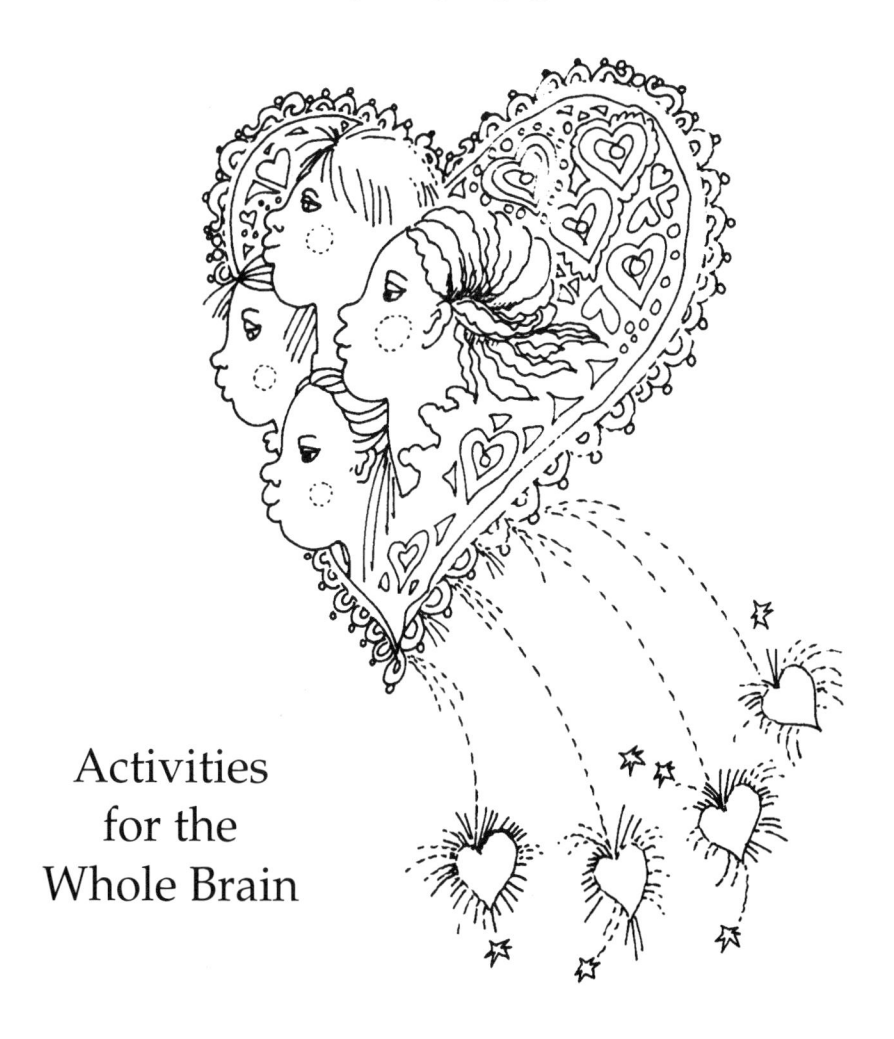

Activities for the Whole Brain

On the next page, outline the large square
with your animal's colors.
(Green, Blue, Yellow or Red)

If your largest growth ring is Blue,
outline the Look-about square.
Then INSIDE this Blue square,
outline the square which shows you
your second largest growth ring.

If your second largest ring is Yellow,
then outline the small Talk-about square
INSIDE the large Look-about square.

Let's look at the Value words.
Look at the smaller square you outlined
which shows your second largest growth ring.
Do the value words seem familiar
and important to you?
These are your deeply-rooted values —
your emotional core.

There's a lot to learn from understanding
our deeply-rooted values. When we feel whole in these
four different ways, we know how thought,
experience and feeling values fit together.
Though each of us is more like one or two of them,
we can learn from all four.

Think-about Values
Look-about values

Order **Facts** **Safety**	Look-about Freedom Choices Results	Think-about Order Facts Safety	**Freedom** **Choices** **Results**
Feel-about Harmony Belonging Hands-on	Talk-about Understanding Ideas Creativity	Feel-about Harmony Belonging Hands-on	Talk-about Understanding Ideas Creativity
Think-about Order Facts Safety	Look-about Freedom Choices Results	Think-about Order Facts Safety	Look-about Freedom Choices Results
Harmony **Belonging** **Hands-on**	Talk-about Understanding Ideas Creativity	Feel-about Harmony Belonging Hands-on	**Under-** **standing** **Ideas** **Creativity**

Feel-about values
Talk-about values

When all the parts work together well, something happens called Synergy. When the four selves work together to solve problems, they are truly close synergy pals. Interdependence is different and more valued than independence.

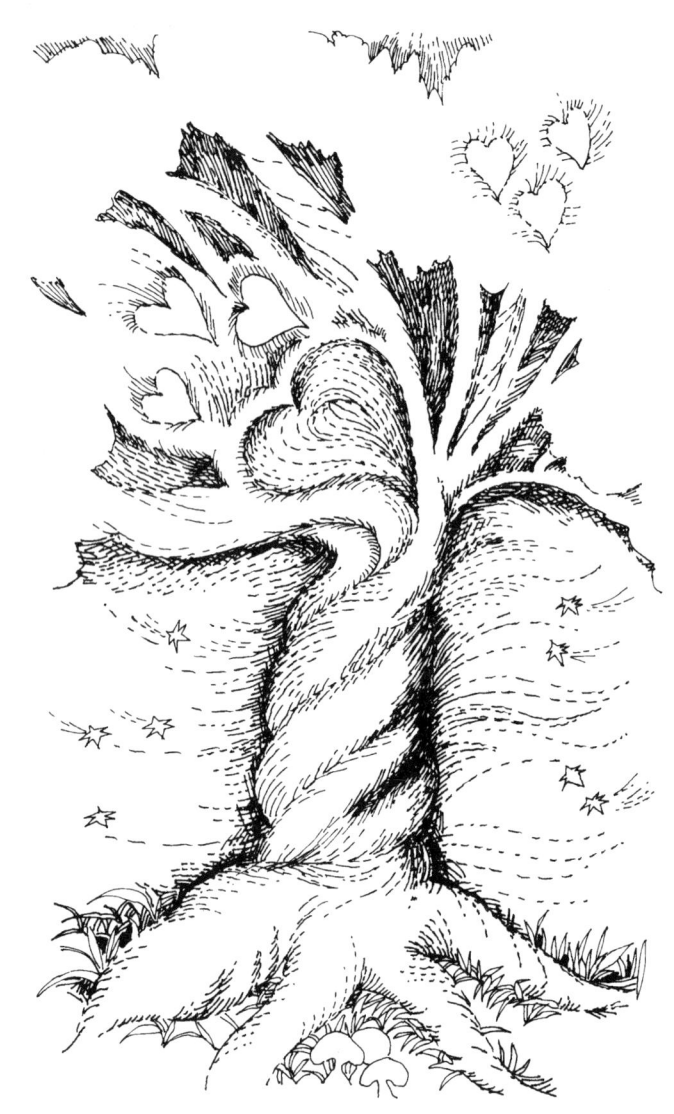

"Wisdom is the tree of Life to those who embrace her; those who lay hold of her will be blessed."
                    Proverbs 3.18 NIV

Working Together as
Synergy Pals

When each is a part of the whole

Did you see a little bit of all the Think-about, Look-about, Talk-about, Feel-about parts in yourself — the parts close to your heart?

All About You in the Creative Circle

When we learn from all four of our special selves, rather than just one or two all the time then all the parts work together easily and well, and all contribute their natural talents at the right time.

Then something happens called SYNERGY.

When the four selves work together to know what you want, to solve problems, all the time, in the right way, they are truly SYNERGY PALS.

Then they can work together for a PURPOSE.

The Owl, the Lion, the Chimp and Koala
learn how to stay healthy, and have fun,
through all of the work and the play,
one and all, every day.
Each is a part of the whole.

The Lion, the Chimp, the Koala and Owl
all name their troubles, and tell themselves,
"Now I'll learn from the rest and can be
my best
when I am part of the whole."

The Chimp, the Koala, the Owl and Lion
learn lots from each other
when they try on each other's feelings.
It really is healing, seeing each as part of
the whole.

The Koala, the Owl, the Lion and Chimp
all learn how to be loving.
And to make it simple,
they each give their best to all of the rest,
when each is part of the whole.

Think-about Owl's Natural Talents

Order
Facts
Safety

"Once we get all the facts in order, we'll know the best way to do things."

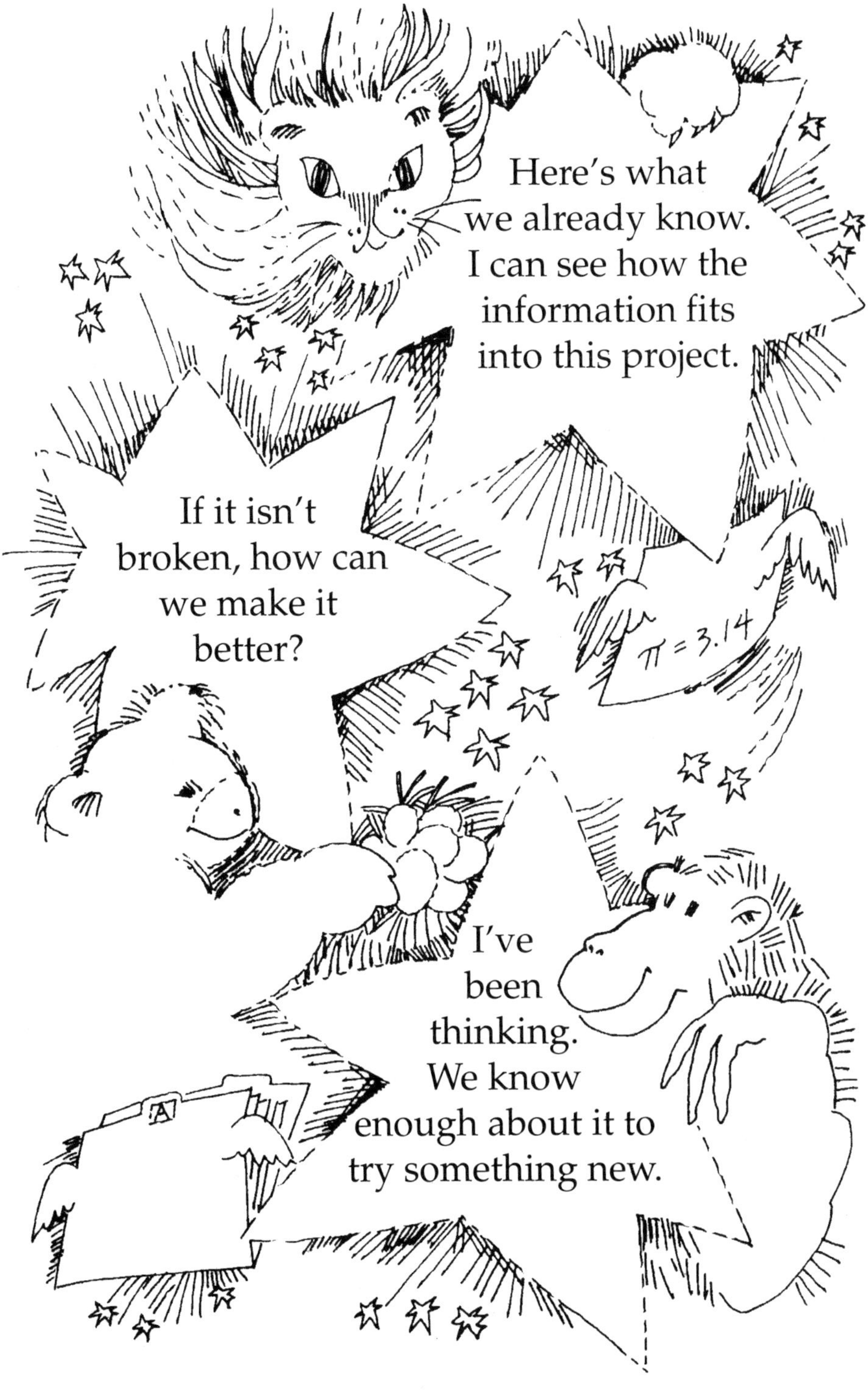
Here's what we already know. I can see how the information fits into this project.
If it isn't broken, how can we make it better?
I've been thinking. We know enough about it to try something new.
π = 3.14
A

Look-about Lion's Natural Talents

Freedom
Choices
Results

"We'll get somewhere only if we choose what we want to have happen."

I've looked at the problem totally and carefully. Here's what we can do.
Let's make a model to see if the material will work.
I understand what we're trying to do. There may be more than one way to do it.

Talk-about Chimp's Natural Talents

Understanding Ideas Creativity

"Let me tell you about this fantastic new idea. Tell me what you think of it."

Let's play with it and see what happens if we do it differently.

Given what we know is true, it's possible that . . .

Let's find out what's on the other side of that mountain.

Feel-about Koala's Natural Talents

Harmony
Belonging
Hands-On

"I made it just for you; I knew you'd like it."

You have to handle things with just the force they need. Not more or less.

It's okay the way it is, but let's move a few things around a little. It won't hurt it.

We can build it together, if we all lend a hand.

Think-about Owl knows your need for order and doing things the right and safe way.

Look-about Lion knows your need for freedom and doing things your own way.

All About You

Feel-about Koala knows your need for harmony and doing things easily together.

Talk-about Chimp knows your need for understanding and doing things in a new and fun way.

Study this chart for clues about how each part of you
is doing what it does best.

Earth Keeper finds the right way	Star Leader shapes the way out
Peace Maker loves the easy way	Dream Mover seeks a new fun way

When these close pals team up and work together
in different ways, they show us
how we use our strengths to act in the world.
When we see how the whole works,
we can achieve much more working together —
serving others, leading, being in action and becoming
someone, so the new can take place.

When I am a Think-about Owl
I Need Time to Figure it Out

I FEEL	Cornered and Stubborn
WHEN	You push or criticize me
BECAUSE	I value Order and conformity I need a quiet, safe place
LESSON	RISK starting without rules or all the facts
SHARE	My feelings and be kind
STRETCH	My boundaries for having fun

When I am a Feel-about Koala
I Need to be a Part of the Group

I FEEL	Left out
WHEN	What I feel and do doesn't seem to matter
BECAUSE	I value Harmony I need to be a part of what's going on
LESSON	RISK being honest about my needs and feelings
SHARE	My decisions, expectations, dreams
STRETCH	To challenge myself and take charge

When I am a Look-about Lion
I Need to Act on Plans and Direct

I FEEL	Blocked
WHEN	You avoid decision and follow-through action
BECAUSE	I value Freedom to act I need to do new things and get results
LESSON	RISK being fun-loving while working slower
SHARE	and listen to your feelings and words
STRETCH	to be considerate and accept what others offer

When I am a Talk-about Chimp
I Need to Question and Communicate

I FEEL	Misunderstood
WHEN	You don't listen to my inspired ideas or share my playful mood
BECAUSE	I value Understanding I need to direct myself ; question's are okay to seek the new rules
LESSON	RISK losing inspiration with organization
SHARE	the work
STRETCH	to plan ahead and finish it step by step

Did you discover some interesting things about your natural talents? Did you learn about your troubles and the life lessons they teach? All the discovering we do helps us understand how to live with ourselves and others.

The links of our past experiences give us clues that will vary with each of us. However, the same promise to be recognized calls each of us, as we learn about our natural talent in the creative circle of learning.

Living with other people can be difficult and painful if we don't know ourselves very well. We may see ourselves as separate and lonely instead of connected. Could it be the reason support feels so good is because it's the way human beings are *supposed* to do things? Interdependence gives more than independence.

What happens when someone tries to be something he or she isn't? If we are set in our ways with strong beliefs, we expect others to be the same as we are and we can get angry and hurtful. If we try to be like other people want us to be all the time, we hide our true selves Inside and feel squashed and nervous.

How each is a part of the Whole

The living whole tree reaches for light and grows. The whole world is a circle of thought reaching for the light of understanding. Old roots and new rules tell us that we need to learn how to work together to be whole.

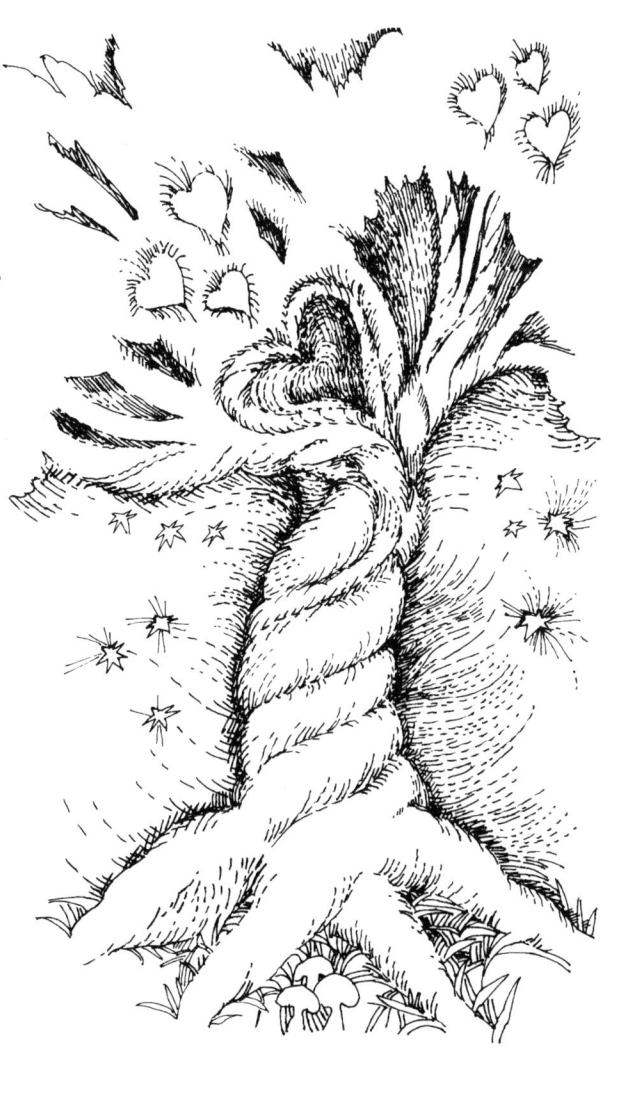

English
Tomorrow when school is out, I plan to buy a little pumpkin for myself.

1970 October
Peter

Seven Stretches

I Need to Keep the Growing Edge Healthy

Where are you in your understanding of the riddle of You? Think about where you feel your own growth reaches. Are you a tiny tree with a lot of growing to do? Or have you grown a lot already? Although we can never completely know and understand another person's map of the world, we can all increase our awareness of the differences.

What is not Synergistic

Too much sameness = no creative action

Too much difference = no agreement

Too much misdirected natural talent = burn out

Too few natural talents for the project = frustration and anger

How many oak trees are there in an acorn?

1) I can accept that there are unknowns in life...
Choices - I know I can be myself and make up my mind in my own time, even if I'm different from others.

Disappointments - I can feel okay, even if I don't always understand what's going on around me. I can learn by looking at it.

Relationships - I can accept other people the way they are without needing to put them down. I can appreciate natural differences.

Is It More Me or Someone Else . . .

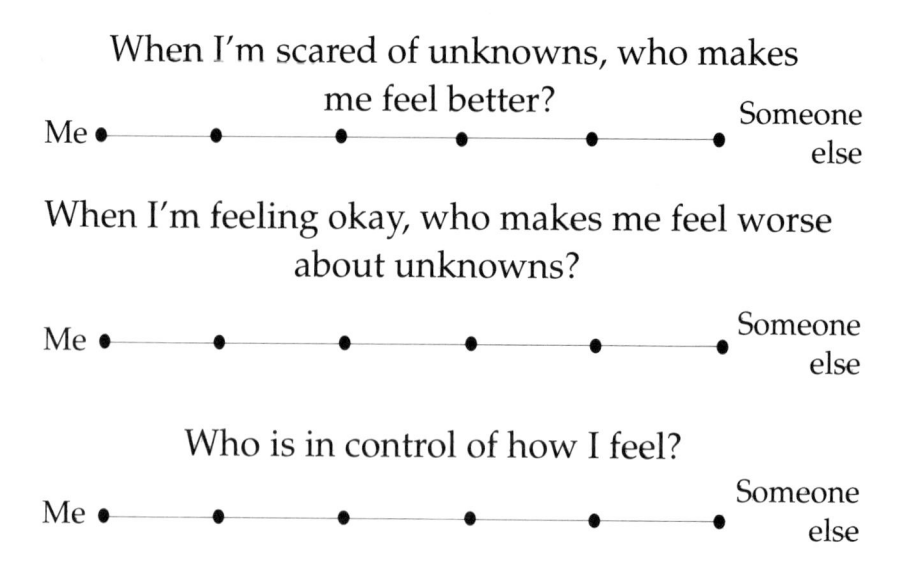

When I'm scared of unknowns, who makes me feel better?

Me •—————•—————•—————•—————•—————• Someone else

When I'm feeling okay, who makes me feel worse about unknowns?

Me •—————•—————•—————•—————•—————• Someone else

Who is in control of how I feel?

Me •—————•—————•—————•—————•—————• Someone else

These are the unknowns I can accept in my life:

2) I can accept to stay open to new information and ideas...

Choices - I can change my opinion, given new information. I can consider new ideas and evaluate them as possibilities.

Disappointments - I can admit my errors in thinking and change AND allow others to do the same.

Relationships - I'm willing to listen to what others have to say. I don't need to make others agree with me.

Is It More Me or Someone Else . . .

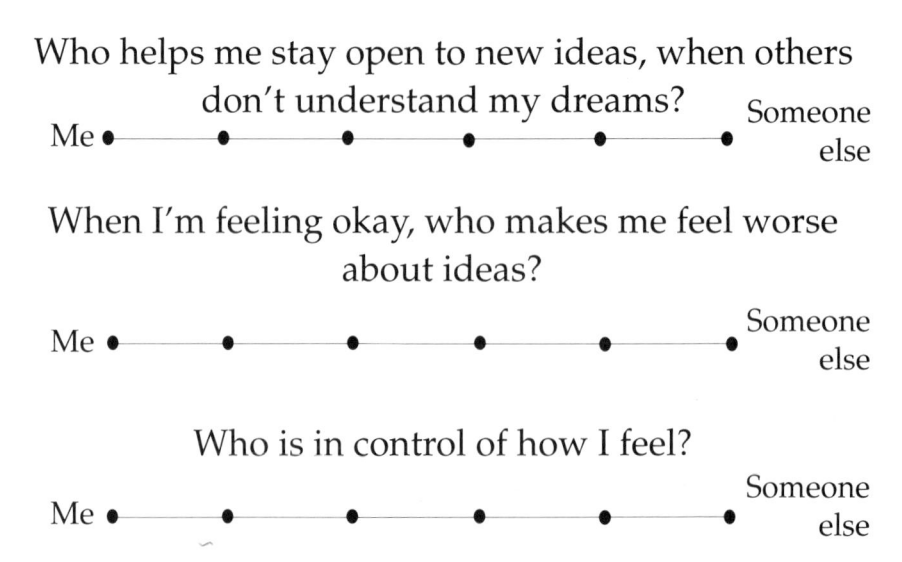

Who helps me stay open to new ideas, when others don't understand my dreams?

Me •———•———•———•———•———• Someone else

When I'm feeling okay, who makes me feel worse about ideas?

Me •———•———•———•———•———• Someone else

Who is in control of how I feel?

Me •———•———•———•———•———• Someone else

New information and ideas in my life are…

_____

_____

_____

_____

3) I can talk about what hurts in helpful ways, instead of repressing my words and thoughts.

Choices - I can choose my words and tone of voice to really communicate and say what I mean.

Disappointments - I can expand my range of expression so that others can get my meaning better. I can learn from their misunderstandings.

Relationships - I can listen to and respect what others are trying to say to me. I can understand our natural differences of expression and perception.

Is It More Me or Someone Else . . .

Who helps me to decide that it's safe to talk about what hurts?

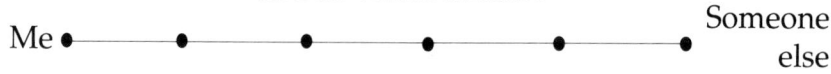

Me •———•———•———•———•———• Someone else

When I'm feeling okay, who makes me feel worse or feel accepted?

Me •———•———•———•———•———• Someone else

Who is in control of how I feel?

Me •———•———•———•———•———• Someone else

How have I been helpful…

_____

_____

_____

_____

4) I can choose to see the good side of things...

Choices - I can be creative in life and look for opportunity.

Disappointments - I can accept that bad things happen to good people. I can learn to look for meaning.

Relationships - I can choose to see the good side of others *and* myself.

Is It More Me or Someone Else ...

Who helps me see the good side of things even when I'm disappointed?

Me •———•———•———•———•———• Someone else

When I'm feeling okay, who makes me feel worse or sees my sucesses?

Me •———•———•———•———•———• Someone else

Who is in control of how I feel?

Me •———•———•———•———•———• Someone else

The good side of things in my life now are…

_____

_____

_____

_____

5) I can choose to see the funny side of life...

Choices - I can choose to see life's experiences as an amusing story.

Disappointments - With a sense of humor, I can learn to see the funny side of any setback.

Relationships - I can laugh and learn from my own experiences, and laugh with — not at — others.

Is It More Me or Someone Else . . .

Who helps me see the funny side of things?

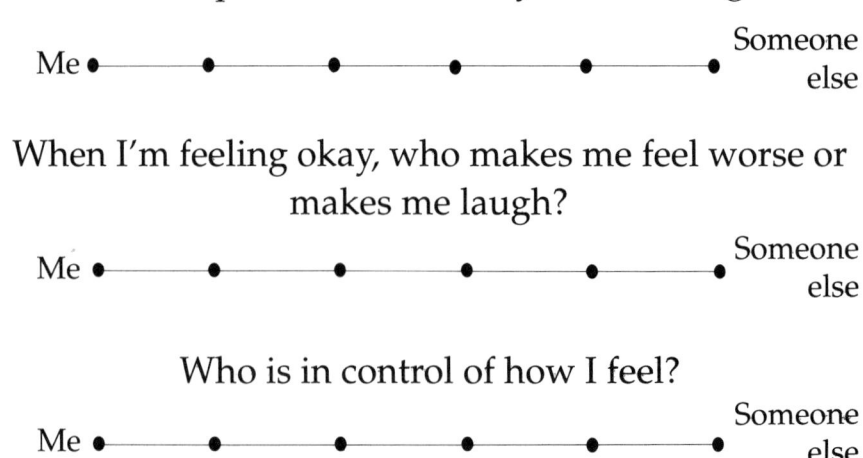

Me •——•——•——•——•——• Someone else

When I'm feeling okay, who makes me feel worse or makes me laugh?

Me •——•——•——•——•——• Someone else

Who is in control of how I feel?

Me •——•——•——•——•——• Someone else

The funny things in my life now are…

_____

_____

_____

_____

6) I can choose to look at details without losing sight of the big picture or plan...

Choices - I can seek out ideas and information step-by-step to solve problems in unusual and creative ways.

Disappointments - I can learn lots from acting too quickly on a project that I don't know how to finish.

Relationships - I can understand the benefits of synergy by working with others who have different talents than I do.

Is It More Me or Someone Else . . .

Who helps me follow through on the details?

Me •―――•―――•―――•―――•―――• Someone else

When I'm feeling okay, who makes me feel worse or okay about details?

Me •―――•―――•―――•―――•――――• Someone else

Who is in control of how I feel?

Me •―――•―――•―――•―――•――――• Someone else

Important details in my life now are…

_____

_____

_____

_____

7) I can accept my own truth while looking at my surroundings with an open mind…

Choices - I can do what I think is right, not just what others want me to do. I can look at other ways of doing things, and choose to be courageous.

Disappointments - I can see that my fears seem real and drive me away from pain towards the pleasure of learning something important.

Relationships - I set my own boundaries and take care of myself when others do things I don't want to do, becoming more self-reliant and dependent on myself.

Is It More Me or Someone Else . . .

Who helps me see my own true cycles of growth?

Me •———•———•———•———•———• Someone else

When I'm feeling okay, who makes me feel worse or okay about what's true for me?

Me •———•———•———•———•———• Someone else

Who is in control of how I feel?

Me •———•———•———•———•———• Someone else

New truths in my life are…

_____

_____

_____

_____

A Good Fit With Others?
Where do you stand on the line?

1) Starting from the center dot, mark an (X) along the line where you feel in control of your own expectations.
2) Mark a (√) on what *other* people expect of you.
3) Draw a line between the (X), your expectations, and the (√), other's expectations of you.
4) Weaknesses are just exaggerated strengths. Too much safety = too little risk-taking.

I feel: (X) • • • • • • • • • • Others expect: (√)

Are you more comfortable being:

Creative — — — — — — — — — — **Orderly**
High Risk   Low Risk

Do you feel conflict when there is:

Difference — — — — — — — — — — **Sameness**
Disagreement   Agreement
High creativity   Low creativity

Do you feel tension when you have:

Self-directed expectations — — — — — — **Other-directed expectations**
High Self-control   Low Self-control

Do you feel strain when:

Many Natural Talents fit the project — — — — **Too few Natural Talents fit the project**
Fast paced   Slow paced

Do you feel frustration when:

Others expect too much — — — — — — **Others expect too little**

What do I and others expect from me?

How long the line between **X** and √ shows how different expectations can be. A short line means you quickly adapt to change. With a longer line, you need to be gently guided or create small steps in order to stem fears. Understanding differences will change your thinking, feelings and behavior. Seeing each one equal yet different in the creative circle allows more choices for you to work with others. Trying to change others along your line has never worked.

Stretching Your Growing Edge

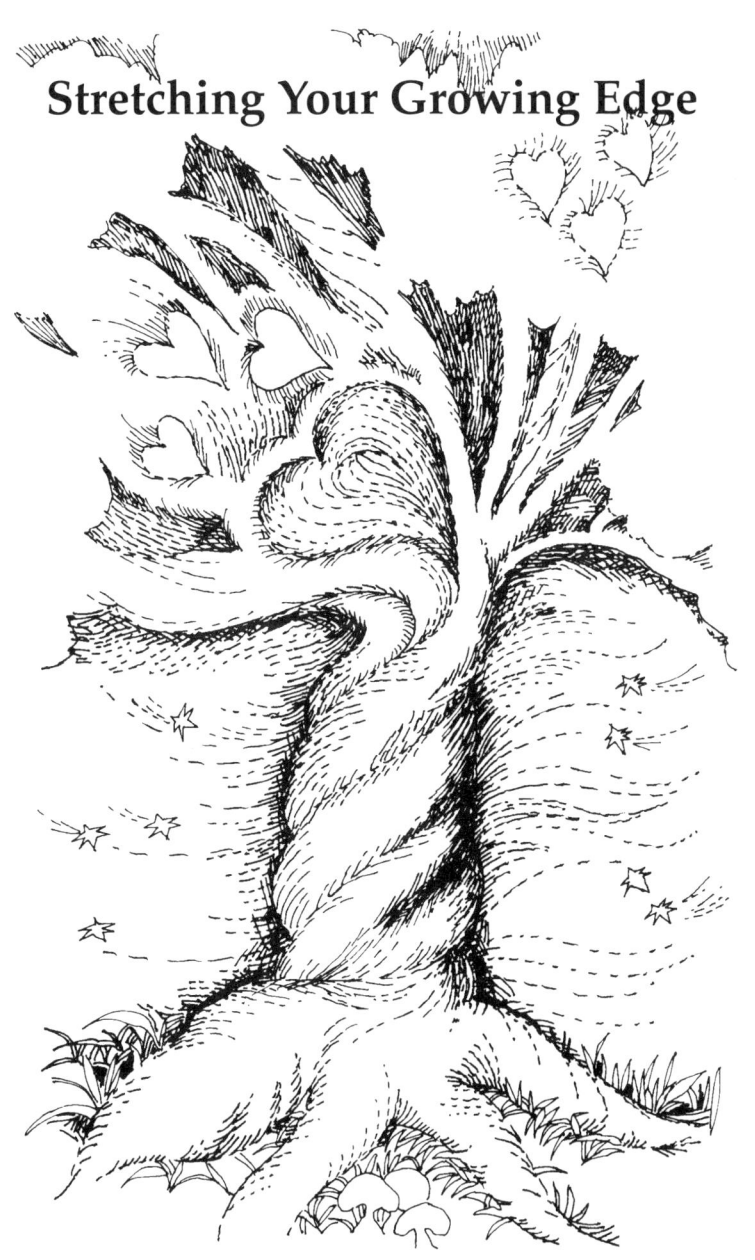

The whole tree reaches for light and grows into a circle of creative thought reaching for a new light of understanding. We need each other to be a whole mind.

Think-about Owl

**When threatened
I may act . . .**

Stoney
Picky
Deliberate
Bored
Stubborn
Suspicious

. . . because I feel bad.

**I need to learn
how to . . .**

Express my feelings
Be spontaneous
Just get started
Enjoy unstructured time
Get along with active people
Trust others decisions

. . . to feel good.

Feel-about Koala

**When threatened
I may act . . .**

Lonely
Afraid
Gullible
Sneaky
Guilty
Impulsive

. . . because I feel bad.

**I need to learn
how to . . .**

Be independent
Be honest about feelings
Be assertive
Be confident
Follow through
To know my boundaries,
finish my goal

. . . to feel good.

Look-about Lion

**When I'm threatened
I may act...**

Bossy
Blunt
Unfeeling
Serious
Demanding
Like I "know it all"

...because I feel bad.

**I need to learn
how to...**

Not be so demanding
Consider others' needs
Listen to feelings
Be more fun and creative
Relax and slow down
Poke fun at myself, and
laugh with others

...to feel good.

Talk-about Chimp

**When I'm threatened I
may act...**

Scattered
Let-down
Overwhelmed
Pushy
Naïve
Worried

...because I feel bad.

**I need to learn
how to...**

Organize details
Follow through; focus
Plan ahead
Listen to others
Be practical
Delegate jobs

...to feel good.

Activities to help me understand how to do things better that are hard for me

Think-about activities | ## Look-about activities

* Assemble a model plane by reading the instructions * Walk instead of ride * Organize your room * Be exactly on time all day * Make an A B C list of things to do	* **Plan and start a business** * **Interview an expert** * **Learn how to run a new computer program** * **Write and direct a play** * **Take charge of a group**
* Dance to the rhythm of the beat * Compose a piece of music * Go back to a sad memory and change the feeling to a happy one * Act quickly for someone in need * Do something nice for yourself	* **Be in a sandcastle contest** * **Discover the hidden meaning in a totem** * **Be in a parade** * **Celebrate & perform** * **Share your daydreams**

Feel-about activities | ## Talk-about activities

Problem Solving with Four Synergy Pals

**Think-about Owl
Skill Master**

Facts
(Needs order to feel good)

- Looks OK
- Worse case checked
- Facts & numbers OK
- Feels safe & sure

**Look-about Lion
Vision Leader**

Plan
(Needs decision to feel good)

- Some potential risks
- Follow-through plan
- Get expert advice
- Knowledge & competence

4 Ways to make sense of a "Whole" Idea

Action
(Needs action to feel good)

- Feels good
- Connects all the parts
- Fulfillment
- Synergy

Brainstorm
(Needs ideas to feel good)

- Terrific ideas
- Best case
- Sixth sense
- Future success

**Feel-about Koala
Peace Maker**

**Talk-about Chimp
Dream Mover**

I Will Most Likely

Tried and True	Up in Space
Think-about Digital Learners	**Look-about Visual Learners**
* Want to do things "right" and by the book	* Learn by seeing and watching demonstrations
* Strive for accuracy and quality, not quickness	* Learn by reading — like descriptions and concentration
* Look at a person's past as a key to trusting them in the future	* Learn spelling — recognize words by sight
* Want clearly-defined tasks, limited risk, and an "open door" policy	* Learn by writing — handwriting is good when young
* Can be very creative in designing helpful systems if encouraged and allowed to work at own pace	* Put things away when finished — do not like clutter
	* Notice details — loves knowledge
* Are good at taking things apart, they *can also* take people apart and become strong critics when wronged	* Like to keep written records
	* Put models together correctly using written directions
* Want their boundaries to be valued and recognized and safe	* Review for tests by writing a summary or reading notes
* Like a cupful of sharpened pencils, things in neat order	* Like lots of eye contact
* knows natural patterns in nature	* Likes' color ' dressing, b eautiful accessories

Do My Best Work

Idea Starter | Down to Earth

Talk-about Auditory Learners | **Feel-about Kinesthetic Learners**

* Learn through verbal instructions from others or self

* Enjoy dialogue and plays, often move lips or subvocalize

* Like to talk a lot and are good storytellers

* Like to sing and enjoy music

* Use mature language

* Learn telephone numbers and addresses quite young

* Like to play with words and make up rhymes

* Good dancers and drummers, have a good sense of rhythm

* May talk to themselves when working alone

* Ask questions about written instructions

* Review for a test by reading aloud or reviewing with others

---

* Learn by doing — hands-on experiences

* Prefer stories where action occurs early

* Often are poor spellers

* Like to touch everything

* Make things out of paper

* Enjoy sports; are well — coordinated

* Like to take things apart and put them back together

* Are prone to fight rather than talk things out

* Like to draw and doodle, and enjoy art projects

* Are usually outdoors kind of people

* Spend time on crafts and shop-type activities

* Prefer movement games

I Can Understand Myself and Others

Now I can understand myself and others.
I know how I like best to do things.

I know now that change is okay, too. I'm not afraid to learn new things or grow, because I know it's perfectly all right to do something different if I want to.

If I have troubles, I know I always have a safe place within myself with my four special selves who will always be there to guide me and help me feel that working and belonging together is the wonder of life.

When I understand myself, I understand my friends, too, because I see a bit of everyone in myself. That will make my journey through life an interesting trip.

All about me and all about you, the friendly universe nourishes and encourages us.

Order, freedom, understanding and harmony turn the creative circle in the friendly universe
and it continues on and on . . .

All About You

Looking at others in a new light of understanding

Resource Words for Adults
Glossary

This glossary not only defines words used in special ways in the book, but adds additional, more technical words and explains how these concepts are portrayed in *All About You*.

Adaptive — One's ability to adjust to circumstances; how the *synergy-about-you-pals*™ work as a team to find appropriate methods to tackle problems in collaboration.
Affiliate — The need of people to associate with one another. In synergistic terms, learning to work harmoniously as a team, balancing tolerances and biases.
Anchor — A stimulus arising from experience that when applied elicits a specific response — pain or pleasure.
Anxiety — Vague apprehension or fear about the future.
Auditory — Using one's ears as the primary way to perceive the world and access information.
Away From — A preference to move in a reverse direction away from pain perceived as someone or something.
Belief — A general expectation or assumption about the way the world operates or other people behave. Beliefs are usually based on one's experience, temperament, and values. Beliefs are learned and can be unlearned or changed.
Communication — Exchanging information using verbal or written language and/or a variety of behavior signals.
Content — The subject matter of events of life and/or interaction with others around which process happens (see also Process).
Decision — The result of using the 7-step process to analyze and determine one's goals and plans for achievement. De-cide means to cut off, move away from pain to pleasure.
Digital — Using language as the primary way to perceive the world and access information.
Dissociation — Having a memory without being connected with the feelings associated with the remembered experience.
Ecology — The study of how the individual affects the whole, the whole affects the individual, and the total relationship between an individual and his or her outer environment. Internal ecology is concerned with the relationship among one's values, beliefs, expectations, and behaviors.
Extrovert — One whose behavior is oriented more in an outward direction, toward other people and external circumstances, in alignment.
Gestalt — The whole picture, the breadth and depth within which one usually focuses more narrowly. It is when one can see the "whole" that the "detail" can be kept in perspective.
Inertia — An impulse to remain in a given state, one's comfort zone, resulting in lack of challenge and growth.

Introvert — One whose behavior is oriented more in an inward direction, concerned with internal conditions.

Kinesthetic — Using one's feeling and touching senses as the primary way to perceive the world and access information.

Language — There are two levels of language: In addition to one's accustomed verbal means of communication (speaking and hearing words), language also refers to different individual "thinking languages," internal/mental communication, which may be visual, auditory, kinesthetic, or analytical.

Learning Styles — An individual's preferred means of acquiring and remembering new information (see Auditory, Digital, Kinesthetic and Visual).

Map — see Paradigm.

Matcher/Matching — Comparing input with known information to determine if it is harmonious or not.

Metaphor — A story that conveys a deeper meaning, that symbolizes how something works or what it means. The "Synergy Tree" story is a metaphor.

Paradigm — A map, framework, or pattern on which to base a belief system. For example, the world was once thought to be flat and then known to be round; the change in how one thought about the round world was a paradigm shift.

Part — A portion of one's personality — for example, the "parts" of Owl, Chimp, Koala, and Lion within each individual.

Process — The growing, changing, evolving that happens around the content of events and interaction with others (see also Content).

Rapport — The sense of trust, compatibility and harmony established between people.

Representational Systems — The five senses (sight, hearing, touch, smell, taste) used to convey information to the brain.

State — The sum total of what one thinks, feels and does at any given time. How emotions are managed may be dependent upon the circumstances of the moment.

Synergy — The effect of how interaction of heterogenous parts multiplies the whole, which becomes more than just the sum of the parts. All life is related; each of us connected to one another, unique, yet more alike than different; a partnership.

Temperament — One's natural method of action or behavior based on personality parts; for example, an individual may behave primarily as a Think-about Owl, but has also Talk-about Chimp, Look-about Lion, and Feel-about Koala aspects to his or her behavior, feisty, fearful, feeling or flexible are anthropomorphic metaphors.

Toward — A preference to move closer to pleasure associated with someone or something.

Value — One's individual (or a group's) values against which people and events are measured as worthwhile or useless. (Order, Freedom, Understanding, Harmony)

Visual — Using one's eyes as the primary way to perceive the world and access information.

Recommended Reading for Adults

The books suggested here are a varied representation of the many that could be recommended.

Aburdene, Patricia; and Naisbett, John, *MEGATRENDS FOR WOMEN*, Villard Books, 1992.

Bandler, Richard, *USING YOUR BRAIN-FOR A CHANGE*, Real People Press, 1985.

Bandler, Richard and Grinder, John, *PATTERNS OF THE HYPNOTIC TECHNIQUE OF MILTON H. ERICKSON, M.D., VOL. 1*, Meta Publications, 1975.

Bandler, Richard; Grinder, John and Satir, Virginia, *CHANGING WITH FAMILIES*, Science and Behavior Books, 1976.

Berends, Polly Berrien, *WHOLE CHILD/WHOLE PARENT*, Harper & Rowe, 1983.

Buzan, Tony, *MAKE THE MOST OF YOUR MIND*, Simon & Schuster, 1984.

Campbell, Joseph, *THE HERO WITH A THOUSAND FACES*, Pantheon, 1949

Chopra, Deepak, M.D., *PERFECT HEALTH*, Harmony, 1990.

Clark & Clark, *HASSLE-FREE HOMEWORK*, Doubleday, 1989.

Crum, Thomas, *THE MAGIC OF CONFLICT*, Simon & Schuster, 1987.

De Bono, Edward, *DE BONO'S THINKING COURSE*, Facts on File Publications, 1985.

Dyer, Wayne, Ed.D., *YOU'LL SEE IT WHEN YOU BELIEVE IT*, William Morrow and Co., 1989.

Ferguson, Marilyn, *THE AQUARIAN CONSPIRACY: PERSONAL AND SOCIAL TRANSFORMATION IN THE 1980s*, J.P. Tarcher, 1987.

Ferris, Timothy, *THE MIND,S SKY: HUMAN INTELLIGENCE IN A COSMIC CONTEXT*, Bantam Books, 1992.

Gilligan, Carol, *IN A DIFFERENT VOICE: PSYCHOLOGICAL*

THEORY AND WOMAN'S DEVELOPMENT, Harvard, 1982.

Hoff, Benjamin, *THE TAO OF POOH*, E.P. Dutton, 1982.

Illich, Ivan, *DESCHOOLING SOCIETY*, Harper & Row, 1871.

Jung, Carl, *MAN AND HIS SYMBOLS*, Doubleday, 1964.

Jung, Carl, *PSYCHOLOGICAL TYPES*, Pantheon, 1953.

Keirsey, David and Bates, Marilyn, *PLEASE UNDERSTAND ME: AN ESSAY ON TEMPERAMENT STYLES*, Prometheus Nemesis, 1978.

Krishnamurti, J., *LIFE AHEAD*, Harper & Row, 1963.

Laborde, Genie, *INFLUENCING WITH INTEGRITY*, Syntony Press, 1986.

L'Engle, Madeleine, *A WRINKLE IN TIME*, Ariel, 1962.

Mische, Gerald and Patricia, *TOWARD A HUMAN WORLD ORDER*, Paulist Press, 1977.

Myers, Isabel Briggs and Peter, *GIFTS DIFFERING*, Consulting Psychologists Press, 1980.

Neustadt, Richard E., *THINKING IN TIME: THE USES OF HISTORY FOR DECISION-MAKERS*, Free Press, 1988.

Ray, Michael and Myers, Rochelle, *CREATIVITY IN BUSINESS*, Doubleday, 1989.

Rico, Gabrielle, *WRITING THE NATURAL WAY: USING RIGHT BRAIN TECHNIQUES TO RELEASE YOUR EXPRESSIVE POWERS*, J.P. Tarcher, 1983.

Robbins, Anthony, *UNLIMITED POWER*, Fawcett Columbine, 1986.

Russell, Peter, *THE GLOBAL BRAIN*, J.P. Tarcher, 1983.

Smith, Lendon, M.D., *IMPROVING YOUR CHILD'S BEHAVIOR CHEMISTRY*, Shaw/Spelling Associates, Inc., 1989.

SmithChurchland, Patricia, *THE COMPUTATIONAL BRAIN, 1992*

Sternberg, Robert J., ed., *THE NATURE OF CREATIVITY*, Cambridge, 1988.

Tavris, Carol, *THE MISMEASURE OF WOMEN*, Random House, 1992.

Weisberg, Robert, *CREATIVITY, GENIUS AND OTHER MYTHS*, W.H. Freeman, 1986.

Everyone you know should have a copy of
All About You:
In The Creative Circle

No. 1

by Ardys U. Reverman
@ $14.95 each
Phone Order Line

1- 503 228 6463

(MasterCard and VISA)
FAX Order Line: (503) 241-2516

BOOKS	CASES	UNIT PRICE
1-4	——	$14.95 Each
5-23	——	$12.95 Each
24	1 ($113.40)	$9.45 Each
288	12 (1995.00)	$6.95 Each
Circle 1 & Teamwork 2		$24.95 Pair
Roots 3 & Search 4		$39.95 Set

Shipping and handling (inside USA) add 5%.
Add area sales tax if applicable.
(Outside USA) add 10%.

EMPOWER YOURSELF AND OTHERS WITH THIS BOOK!
In The Creative Circle *is the positive thinking tool of the '90s*

How To:
- Use this breakthrough handbook (which no parent or teacher can afford to ignore).
- Use an easy, self-help quiz for a quick "snapshot" of your motivations.
- Move your family from pieces to peace with obstacle resolution skills.
- Understand healthy ways to respond to setbacks.

Shipping: ($2.00 for 1st book + .75¢ for each additional book ordered)
TOTAL AMOUNT ENCLOSED: _____

Send check or money order to:
TAPROOTS PRESS
3503 SW Gale Avenue
Portland, OR 97201

PLEASE ADD MY NAME TO THE TAPROOTS PRESS QUARTERLY NEWSLETTER, SO I MAY RECEIVE MORE INFORMATION ABOUT CREATIVITY AND TEMPERAMENT First issue free and Synergy Poster

No. 1

first issue free (yearly subscription $20.00)
COMPANY NAME:_____
NAME:_____
ADDRESS:_____
CITY:_____STATE:_____ZIP:_____

THE FRIENDLY UNIVERSE THANKS YOU FOR YOUR ORDER!
I cannot wait 3-4 weeks for Book Rate. Here is $4.00 for Air Mail.
Group, class and lecture rates available.
Simply supply us with a name and address to forward books as a gift.
Families are making a change, but it's not a revolution; it's an evolution.